happy at work, happy at home

**THE GIRL'S GUIDE TO
BEING A WORKING MOM**

happy at work, happy at home

THE GIRL'S GUIDE TO BEING A WORKING MOM

Caitlin Friedman

and Kimberly Yorio

BROADWAY BOOKS

new york

Published in the United States by Broadway Books, an imprint of the Crown
Publishing Group, a division of Random House, Inc., New York.
www.crownpublishing.com

BROADWAY BOOKS and the Broadway Books colophon
are trademarks of Random House, Inc.

Library of Congress Cataloging-in-Publication Data
Friedman, Caitlin.
   Happy at work, happy at home : the girl's guide to being a working mom / by
Caitlin Friedman and Kimberly Yorio.
      p. cm.
   1. Working mothers. I. Yorio, Kimberly. II. Title.

   HQ759.48.F75 2009
   306.874'3—dc22

                                    2008049982

ISBN 978-0-7679-3053-6

PRINTED IN THE UNITED STATES OF AMERICA

Book design by Caroline Cunningham

10 9 8 7 6 5 4 3 2 1

First Edition

Caitlin

This book is for Andrew, Declan, and Taylor, since we're all on this crazy and wonderful ride together!

Kimberly

For Sharyn Yorio, my superstar working mother, who gave 100 percent both at home and the office. I still don't know how she managed to pick me and my friends up from soccer practice every night.

contents

acknowledgments

We can't believe that this is actually our fourth book! As with all of the titles, this one was most definitely a group effort, and we want to take a page to thank each person who helped us get this into the hands of busy working moms everywhere. First and foremost, we want to thank our agent, David Black, who never treats us like the small fish in his very big pond. A shout out to former Broadway editor Ann Campbell who bought this book before she left to raise her baby (ironic, right?!). Thank you to our new editor, Christine Pride, who jumped right in to reorganize our thoughts and pages to help make a book we are proud of. Thanks to the publicity team at Broadway—our old friends, David Drake and Tammy Blake (wow, guys, we've known each other a long time), and our new friend, Rachel Rokicki (who we hear nothing but great things about). A special nod to David Black's foreign-rights geniuses, Susan Raihofer and Leigh Ann Eliseo. As you know, girls, nothing makes us happier than to get our foreign editions. And of course, thank you, Aimee Bianca, who continues to hold down the fort at YC Media while we are holed up writing these books or on the road telling people about them.

Caitlin wants to thank Kim again for making all of it just that much more fun. And Kim says, right back at you, Cait. Without you none of this would have happened.

happy at work, happy at home

THE GIRL'S GUIDE TO BEING A WORKING MOM

introduction

While we were in Seattle during our book tour for *The Girl's Guide to Kicking Your Career into Gear,* a woman approached us after a talk. She looked curious, but we read something slightly hostile in her expression as well.

"So you girls live in New York?" she asked.

We nodded, both wondering where she was headed.

"Wow. Don't you feel terrible leaving your kids?"

Though we felt like just shouting "No!" the truth is much more complicated. We love our kids (Caitlin has toddler twins and Kim's son is in elementary school) and miss them while we're gone. And many days we feel guilty, really guilty, about walking out the door. But this time, we had earned the right to go on the road. We certainly weren't feeling terrible about traveling to promote a book we spent two years writing. Our kids were being cared for by their *fathers* and, frankly, we had earned this time away.

In fact, if we had been completely honest, the woman probably would have been shocked. We *loved* touring for our book and the break it offered. For Caitlin, it was the first time in years that she could sleep uninterrupted and past 6:30 a.m. (when we didn't have to be up to do morning television interviews). And both of us were thrilled with the response the book generated, along with the opportunity to connect with the women we wrote the book to help. Sure, we flew red-eyes, slept in uncomfortable hotel rooms, gave interviews at the crack of dawn, and led lunch and evening workshops (often followed by late dinners with clients), and yet it still *felt* like a vacation.

Crazy? Sadly, not at all.

Working motherhood is tough. Juggling your parental, professional, and spousal responsibilities while occasionally addressing your own needs is no small feat. When we admit we need help and look for support, the first suggestion we hear is work less—as if it's the most obvious and easily done thing in the world and we must be brain damaged not to have thought of it ourselves. Even if we could afford to give up the income and our careers, why would we want to? We love work and believe we are better mothers because of it. Society doesn't ask men to choose between work and family. Why should we?

And to think we've come so far, we working mothers. We are no longer a minority, automatically receiving sideways glances of disapproval—or outright lectures—from friends, family, and colleagues. We are an accepted, important, and driving part of the workforce. We can do as good a job as any childless colleague or married man with a stay-at-home wife. Our daily challenges are now the issues of national and political discussion—the availability of safe and affordable child care, and health care for all children, as well as the endless juggling of family and work.

These are facts, but the reality somehow doesn't connect. The prevailing wisdom in this country remains that you need to make a choice between having a career and raising your kids. The perception remains that after having a child, the professional *you* will change as much as the personal *you*—even if you are the exact same employee you were before.

In 1998 journalist Betty Holcomb wrote a book called *Not Guilty!: The Good News for Working Mothers*, published by Simon & Schuster. It's a substantial and superbly researched book that explores the scientific studies, the media and public's impressions, as well as mothers' perceptions about what a "good mother"'s role in society should be. Her extraordinary research supports that we can work outside the home and still be good mothers. She writes about attitudes that make it harder for women not to feel squeezed all of the time, and of course as you can guess from the title, she writes about the guilt mothers have about going to work while also raising families. It's a great book and not only did we learn a lot, we were really taken aback. Almost everything she wrote more than ten years ago still holds true today. What's going on? Why aren't society's attitudes toward working mothers changing? Why aren't there more resources for working mothers in 2008 to help us feel less time pressed, less racked with guilt, and less overwhelmed by their responsibilities? And perhaps most important: Why do working mothers not only earn less than men but also less than other childless working women?

We wish we had the answers to these questions, but in the absence of a more quickly changing society, we can at least arm you with the tools and strategies to set yourself up for success at work and at home. Working mothers need support. And support is not that easy to come by. If you're not one of the very few who are blessed with an accessible, available, willing, and competent family to help you, you are forced to juggle between paid child care and spousal support. And that's after the baby is born. The challenges begin the day you get pregnant.

How do you schedule doctor's appointments so they don't impact your workday? What if you're suffering from morning sickness? How do you go to work and kick ass when you're too tired to even eat? How can you afford to be out of work on unpaid maternity leave?

Where's the help going to come from? All too rarely from your employer or even your spouse (more on that in Chapter Seven). While we don't want to scare you off because we're just in the introduction and because this book is going to offer a number of solutions for you from women all over the country who are making it work—the sad fact is that working moms are often on their own. So much so that organizations are being founded to help them get support and resources from the federal government like many other industrialized countries around the world already offer.

One of our favorite organizations, MomsRising (momsrising .org), was founded in 2006 to create a more family-friendly America. MomsRising lobbies Congress to make positive changes that actually will help working families, including paid family leave, accessible health care, flexible work policies, and subsidized child care. MomsRising is trying to help America catch up with the rest of the world. And we've got a long way to go.

Check out these scary statistics from their Web site:

- In a Harvard study of over 170 countries, the United States was one of only four nations without any form of paid leave for new mothers. (The others were Liberia, Swaziland, and Papua New Guinea.)
- Women without children make 90 cents to a man's dollar, but mothers make just 73 cents, and single mothers make even less—about 60 cents to a man's dollar.
- Mothers are 79 percent less likely to be hired than equally qualified non-mothers.
- A recent study found that mothers were offered $11,000 lower

starting pay than non-mothers with the same résumé for highly paid jobs, while fathers were offered $6,000 more in starting pay.

- Of the twenty most competitive economies in the world, the United States is the only one that does not require employers to provide paid sick days.

The fact is that these statistics are, yes, pretty dismal, but it's all the more reason for you to be aware of what we're up against and armed with the tools and powers to be the best advocate for yourself and other moms. *Happy at Work, Happy at Home* is designed to give you those critical keys to success. In addition to support (paid or un-), if a working mom can take a long-range view of things and not worry so much about each day, learn to ask for what she wants (and needs), delegate more, communicate well, sell her accomplishments, fight for what she deserves at home and at work, make time for herself, and start saying *no* as much as she says *yes,* then it is possible to have a satisfying career and a thriving family.

We aren't delusional. We know this is a tall order. But this book will offer inspiration and ideas that will make you more successful on every front. It is extremely difficult to keep your career a priority, but it is also essential not to give up your goals and dreams because you are now a mother. We love our work and we love our children. We are not defined by either, but both and this book reflects our experiences and those from more than one hundred other women who choose working motherhood.

In interviews with working moms, children of working women, therapists, human resource professionals, counselors, and career coaches, we offer solutions that work for all involved: the partner, children, boss, employees, and—most of all—*you.*

you've got nine months to get ready

HINT: IT GOES QUICK

Congratulations. You're pregnant or thinking about becoming pregnant. You are about to embark on the scariest and most unique nine months of your life. You've signed up for the pregnancy calendar and you eagerly watch the progress of your growing baby. You've stopped caffeine, alcohol, raw cheeses, and sushi and are busy stuffing your face with fresh vegetables and folic acid. You've bought every book on pregnancy and are busily scouring Web sites for all the news you need to know. In between all of this fun and excitement, you go to work. You, after all, are a career girl—a career girl who is also going to be a mom. You are thrilled by the prospect (and perhaps a little scared) and can't wait to shout it from the rooftops once that third month has passed. But don't start shouting yet. You've got a lot of planning to do first.

This chapter will give you the information and strategies you need to successfully navigate your pregnancy. After reading Chapter One, you will be armed with all the tools you need to go on a work- and worry-free maternity leave. We educate about your rights, the options for child care, and share resources and stories that will sup- port you in this very scary and exhilarating time in your life.

Good luck. The next nine months are going to be a whirlwind.

first things first, know your rights

This can get dense. And as with all legalese, you may just want to skip right over it. Don't. Don't even put it off until later. You absolutely must know your legal rights and options, and here they are.

Many pregnant women and new parents are legally protected in the workplace by two, possibly three, federal laws. The first is the Pregnancy Discrimination Act. The PDA amends Title VII of the Civil Rights Act of 1964, the key U.S. statute that prohibits employ- ment discrimination. The U.S. Equal Employment Opportunity Commission (EEOC, http://www.eeoc.gov/facts/fs-preg.html), the government agency in charge of administering and enforcing the PDA, states: "Discrimination on the basis of pregnancy, childbirth or related medical conditions constitutes unlawful sex discrimina- tion under Title VII. Women affected by pregnancy or related condi- tions must be treated in the same manner as other applicants or employees with similar abilities or limitations."

Under the PDA, which applies to employers that have fifteen or more employees, an employer cannot refuse to hire you because of your "pregnancy-related condition" as long as you can perform the functions of the job. Furthermore, your employer can't single out your pregnancy or pregnancy-related condition (morning sickness, anyone?) to determine your ability to work. You may be running to the bathroom to throw up every thirty minutes, but if you're still getting your work done, then your employer can't discriminate against you. Your employer also cannot stereotype you because you are pregnant. For instance, you can't be assigned different projects, passed up for a promotion, or have responsibilities taken away merely because your boss assumes that you can't do the same work you did before you were pregnant. Of course, if your boss's concerns are based on facts (you simply can't keep up the same quality and quantity of work due to your pregnancy or you've told people you plan to work less after giving birth), that poses a different set of considerations.

Women who have health conditions related to their pregnancy also may be protected under the Americans with Disabilities Act (ADA), the U.S. law that prohibits discrimination against individuals who are disabled, are perceived as being disabled, or have a record of being disabled. This statute, which the EEOC also administers, not only prohibits employers from actively discriminating against qualified individuals who are disabled; it also requires that such employers reasonably accommodate such disabled individuals when the accommodation requested by the employee neither materially alters the job duties nor unduly burdens either the employer or fellow employees.

If you have a health issue related to your pregnancy and it becomes serious enough that it requires you to miss work, modify your work schedule, or take a leave of absence, both the PDA and the ADA mandate that your company treat you as well as any other temporarily disabled employee, including providing modified tasks, alternative assignments, disability leave, or leave without pay. In other words, if you are pregnant and disabled as defined by the ADA, your company's internal employment policies, applicable state short-term disability laws, and health and disability insurance policies (check carefully the definition of "disability" in each case, as it often varies) all kick in. Your employer is prohibited by law from treating you any worse than if you had any other type of serious illness or impairment. So, if your company awards time off or flexible work schedules to people who have medical conditions, it may be required to grant the same rights to women suffering from a pregnancy-related condition.

What happens when you need time off work to give birth and take care of your newborn? What happens if you get put on bed rest before your due date? The big news in 1993 (and not much has changed since then) was the passing of the Family Medical Leave Act, or the FMLA as it's called by the U.S. Department of Labor. According to the Department of Labor Web site (http://www.dol.gov/esa/whd/fmla/):

Covered employers must grant an eligible employee up to a total of twelve workweeks of unpaid leave during any twelve-month period for one or more of the following reasons:

- the birth and care of the newborn child of the employee;
- the placement with the employee of a son or daughter for adoption or foster care;
- to care for an immediate family member (spouse, child, or parent) with a serious health condition; or
- to take medical leave when the employee is unable to work because of a serious health condition.

"Covered employers" are businesses that employ more than fifty people and "eligible employees" include those who have worked at the company for twelve months prior and for at least 1,250 hours of service during the twelve-month period prior to the beginning of the leave. So basically, if you work for a large company for more than one year, the law provides that you can take unpaid leave for twelve workweeks. You generally can take these twelve weeks of leave consecutively or intermittently, even up to a few hours at a time (obstetrician visits, anyone?). Unsurprisingly, there often is quite a bit of bureaucracy and paperwork involved in properly requesting and obtaining FMLA leave, so eligible employees should be sure to check with their human resources (HR) departments and get all of the right information. Then again, if you work at a larger covered employer, you may already be used to loads of paperwork and bureaucracy.

If you work in any other situation and there is no state or local law that covers you (see The Paid-Leave Squeeze on page 14), then you may very well have no legal rights at all. You are likely subject to the policies and, more often than not, the whims of your employer.

Remember the company handbook that you received when you started? Now is the time to dig it out and review the section on short-term disability. Most companies with more than a handful of workers have written policies that apply to sickness, child care/maternity leave, leaves of absence due to disability and short-term disability insurance coverage. Find them and figure out how they mesh together if your employer hasn't done so for you. If you cannot find these materials, get them from your HR department, which is required to give this written information to you. Also, you may want to get on the Web. Check out the information related to your individual state's labor, civil rights, and insurance policies. If your employer's health care or short-term disability insurance carriers have Web sites, pull information from there. When it comes to short-term disability insurance—the likeliest way for you to get at least some pay during maternity leave—results really will vary. What you are entitled to will depend on the state in which you live, the generosity of your employer, and the nature of your pregnancy and delivery. While some states don't even mandate short-term disability insurance, a small handful are particularly generous. While some employers offer only the minimum required by law, some go far beyond—particularly for long-time workers. While some state laws and insurance plans allow more time if you've had complications or a cesarean delivery, many also cover bed rest before birth.

At best, it's a challenge to decipher how your employer treats absences due to pregnancy, pregnancy-related health issues, and childbirth-related leaves. At worst, it can be a complicated and sometimes seemingly contradictory hodgepodge of rules, deadlines, and paperwork. According to www.babycenter.com (Kim's favorite Web site when she was pregnant in 1999), maternity or parental leave becomes a patchwork of short-term disability, sick leave, vacation days, personal days and the legally required unpaid family leave. All of this means that planning is crucial in the early stages of your pregnancy. The goal is to set yourself up with all of the necessary information as soon as possible, so that you can make both a seamless exit and stress-free return to the workplace.

save your time, you're going to need it

As your pregnancy progresses, you will begin to craft a birth plan. You would be smart to create a maternity leave plan, too. Your goal is to maximize the paid time off and it quickly becomes a juggling act. Here are a few ways to stockpile your days:

- Schedule all doctors' appointments for off-work hours. You want to demonstrate to the boss and team that your priority is still the job (even if it isn't).
- Go to work even when you're feeling crappy—provided that you can get the job done. It's better to show up and get something done than use up a sick day that you will need later.
- Do not go to work if you feel so lousy that you can't get your work done. Go to the doctor instead. While you may think

you're being a trouper, you may be giving your boss a good and legally permissible reason to deal with you harshly or treat you differently due to your pregnancy.

· Begin a savings plan—not for the baby's college education—but for when you are making half your pay when you are at home taking care of the baby.

girl talk

Elizabeth is an executive at a major national retailer in her sixth month of pregnancy. She is feeling absolutely great and starting to put her maternity leave plan together. Her company's paid maternity leave is based on years of service, and she is one year shy of the ten-year bonus of extra time off. She's earned eight weeks of paid maternity and two weeks at half-pay. If she has a C-section she will get an extra two weeks pay.

She has four weeks of vacation and plans to use those as a backup if she's not ready, but right now she's planning to come back when the ten weeks are up. She's recently been promoted, so she plans to be available to the staff during her leave. She had a bad experience when one of her colleagues chose "radio silence" as her maternity leave plan, so she plans to be as accessible as she needs to be.

Elizabeth has done everything to ensure that she will have a smooth maternity leave, including planning her delivery to coincide with the quietest time in retail, January. She is planning to be back in the office when things kick off in March. She's hired an additional person to support her number two while she's out and she's hoping for the best.

She does have a few worries, though. Her husband would prefer that she didn't return to work, so she knows there will be a few struggles in the beginning, and second, and wisely, she realizes that she has no idea how she's going to feel and what's going to happen after the baby is born, so her biggest plan is to take a "wait-and-see" attitude. She's planned as much as she can and she's hoping for the best.

the paid-leave squeeze

The United States has the worst record on paid parental leave of all of the developed nations. Our country still operates on the 1950s model of father in the workforce and mother home raising the children. There's no easy answer. As mothers, we see the necessity of paid leave for new mothers, fathers, or caregivers. As business owners, we can't take on the financial load of paying for extended maternity leave without government or employee subsidy. If the law required us to pay fifty-two weeks of maternity leave as they do in the United Kingdom, we'd be out of business. At our small company, we can't afford to pay someone who is not working.

Help is on the way. As of September 2008, California, Washington, and New Jersey have passed "paid-leave" bills and there are movements in a handful of other states, including New York, Massachusetts, and Oregon, to implement paid leave. Many paid-leave advocates are lobbying for time off with pay to be a federal law and program.

A bill introduced in the House in 2008 by Representative Fortney Stark (D-California) would mandate twelve weeks of paid leave. The legislation would be funded by a new federal trust fund. Employers (only companies with fifty or more employees) and employees would pay into this fund equally through payroll deductions, similar to unemployment benefits. A bipartisan bill in the Senate sponsored by senators Chris Dodd (D-Conn.) and Ted Stevens (R-Alaska) calls for eight weeks of paid family leave within a one-year period. Benefits would be paid out on a tiered system, depending on salary.

The paid-leave program in California piggybacks on the state's disability program and is 100 percent funded by the employees themselves at an annual average cost of about $47, depending on salary. Californians who opt-in to the program get 55 percent of their pay while on family leave. Who wouldn't trade $47 dollars per year for twelve weeks of paid leave even at half-pay?

These are small gains for the U.S. worker as compared to other countries around the world. Take Canada. According to Wikipedia, in 2000, parental leave was expanded in Canada from ten weeks to thirty-five weeks, divided as desired between two parents. This is in addition to fifteen weeks maternity leave, giving a total possible period of fifty weeks paid leave for a mother. There is still no paid leave for new fathers, however. In Canada, maternity and parental leave is paid for by their employment insurance system.

how family friendly is your workplace?

Most of us expect that our employers and colleagues will be thrilled when we announce our good news. After all, having a baby is a miraculous and magical event. And while that's true for you, it's certainly not true for your employer. Many employers become downright hostile when you announce your news. They are looking down the road to when you are out on maternity leave or running home to tend to a sick child. But don't be discouraged because there are a growing number of companies that are prioritizing family-friendliness and trying to create a work environment that supports the employee and her changing familial needs.

Every year *Working Mother* magazine selects the "100 Best Companies" for family-friendliness in the country through an intensive application process whereby seven areas of family-friendliness are measured and scored, including workforce profile (how many women work at the company), compensation, child care, flexibility, time off and leaves, family-friendly programs, and company culture. *Working Mother*'s "100 Best" among other things offer their employees financial-planning services, flextime, telecommuting, health-care insurance for part-time workers, child-care resources and referrals, job sharing, lactation programs (designated area), prenatal programs, domestic partner benefits, paid paternity leave beyond the FMLA, and a compressed workweek.

If you're working for a large company, this list is a good place to start to evaluate the family-friendliness of your company. With small companies it's more of a case-by-case situation. As a small business owner, Kim can point to a number of times her "mother guilt" has come not from missing a school play but rather from getting angry when an employee's family responsibilities affected productivity. Your pregnancy and impending motherhood are hard on an employer and you can't assume just because your boss is female that you won't get push-back. As much as Kim is thrilled for you personally when you tell her you're pregnant, the manager in her unfortunately jumps to pregnancy brain, maternity leave, breast-feeding schedules, and ultimately reduced productivity. And Kim is a woman and a mother. Imagine how your male manager will take the news. Even in the most progressive company with the most progressive managers, the truth of family-friendliness emerges the second you announce your pregnancy.

We wish it were as simple as flextime and a softly lit, private area to breast-feed. Corporate culture and politics are a fact of life for pregnant women and mothers. Workplaces become separated into the parents and non-parents (or pregnants and non-pregnants). No one can deny that caregivers (and we're including parents as well as non-parents who are taking care of relatives) have more responsibilities vying for their time and attention than non-caregivers. Caregivers also have different priorities. The job is no longer the only thing in our lives. Web sites and message boards are lit up with complaints on both sides of the issue. The employees, mostly women who don't have children, feel unfairly saddled with assignments that require travel and late nights. Working women with children feel like they have been moved aside as the top performers because of their other responsibilities, which is probably the most obvious factual support for the sad truth that things in the workplace really haven't changed. But being aware of and sensitive to these issues will help you navigate office politics and find ways to work more effectively with your colleagues who have a different reality at home.

IS YOUR WORKPLACE FAMILY FRIENDLY?

Is your office really working-parent friendly? Ask yourself these ten questions. The answers will paint a clearer picture than your human resources manual ever could.

1. Are you the first woman in your organization to become pregnant? Good luck, pioneer. You have an opportunity to create a positive program for those who follow.
2. When other women have shared their pregnancy news, what has been the reaction? Have you noticed griping and gossiping behind her back?
3. Do you sense a feeling that they are happy for your/her news, but really more worried about decreased productivity, maternity leave, and whether or not the women will return from maternity leave.
4. Did management partner with the pregnant woman to make a plan for her maternity leave?
5. Did management and/or coworkers show any interest in the pregnancy or act as if nothing had changed?

6. How did the pregnant woman's role in the organization change when she returned from maternity leave?

7. Did the pregnant woman do all she could to prepare for a smooth exit and return?

8. Is your manager the type who doesn't want you taking sick days even when you're home with the stomach flu?

9. Are there qualified employees in your organization or on your team who can assume some of your duties while you are gone?

10. Are there mothers in senior positions of management?

time to break the news

There's one last piece of research to do before you share your news. Make sure you know your job performance status. More than a few women who have announced their pregnancy have been fired shortly after their announcement for an unrelated issue. Pull out your most recent review if you have one. Investigate how many sick and vacation days you have left. Review your current workload and what it will look like in six months.

Now you're ready. You've consulted the human resources manual. You've taken a good hard look at the culture and put the inevitable off for as long as possible. You are in your second trimester and it's becoming impossible to hide behind loose-fitting clothes. If you don't break the news soon, it's going to get out without you controlling the message. And that is the last thing you want after all of your careful planning.

Schedule a private meeting with your boss and tell her in a professional way that you are indeed pregnant and due in six months. "Your message needs to be, 'I care about this job, and I'm going to do everything I can to make sure things run smoothly while I'm not here,' " says DeAnne Rosenberg, a career consultant in Wareham, Mass., and author of *A Manager's Guide to Hiring the Best Person for Every Job.*

Let her know you would like to tell the team yourself and schedule another meeting to review your workload in a couple of weeks. Tell her that you will be formulating a plan and a recommendation for how the workload can be allocated while you are on maternity leave, but don't make any recommendations until you have constructed a thorough plan. The next section will guide you through how to do just that.

help them help you

What do you do in a day? A week? A month? Write it all down. The goal is to create a written version of your office life that your manager and coworkers can consult while you are out. Include your job description, a calendar with daily, weekly, and/or monthly duties. Some tasks will require step-by-step instructions. Include a list of helpful hints, client information and contact information for vendors, partners, or any other people who could possibly be involved. Schedule training with the person covering for you well in advance of your planned departure. Pregnancy is a very unpredictable condition. One day you're fine and the next could find you getting early contractions and ordered on bed rest. We certainly hope that's not the case, but better safe than sorry. The career advisers on www.monster.com suggest you create a workplace map where you write down (or draw) how someone else can easily navigate your workspace. Make sure regular clients or customers know that you'll be on leave and give instructions as to whom they should contact while you're gone. And finally, set your e-mail to automatically forward to the new temp, your home office, or your supervisor and leave a similar message on your voice mail.

It's best to start "The Book of You" in your second trimester when your mind is still clear and your energy is at its peak. Most of this extra work will have to be done on your own time, and the last thing you want to be doing in your ninth month is staying late drawing a map of your desk!

10 Pregnancy Dos and Don'ts

1. Don't share ultrasounds with your team.
2. Do keep photos on your desk.
3. Don't shop for baby furniture, plan the shower, interview nannies, or research baby names at work.
4. Do maximize your lunch hour for personal errands.
5. Don't take on additional after-work responsibilities.
6. Do offer to take on planning, projects, or meetings that are scheduled during work hours.
7. Don't talk about your excitement about your upcoming work break to coworkers.
8. Do plan your maternity leave carefully.
9. Don't fill everyone in on the directions from your doctor.
10. Do eat and drink throughout the day.

pregnancy brain and other side effects of the happiest time of your life

Pregnant women fall into two camps: those who feel great during their pregnancy and those who don't. Their work lives can be very different. If you're feeling great, there's no reason not to make your work life as rich and full as it was before you were pregnant. And if you're feeling poorly, it's a good idea to try to fake it.

If you're not suffering from morning sickness, you're lucky. More than 50 percent of women do, according to the American Pregnancy Association. You are also exhausted. Even though you want to behave as if nothing has changed, your body betrays you. It is changing every minute during your pregnancy. When Kim was pregnant she fell asleep at 8:30 p.m. every night of her first trimester—and this from a girl who would normally have three or four work or social evening functions a week.

You also get this thing called "pregnancy brain." Information is going in, but processed thoughts aren't coming out. For years men and women have thought it was an excuse that pregnant women were using to cover up for their forgetfulness or odd behaviors. Fortunately, there is now proof from a 2008 study by two Australian researchers for the University of New South Wales. The study, published in *The Journal of Clinical and Experimental Neuropsychology*, found that the memory loss can extend up to a year after birth and was shown to effect new memories more than old. For example, a new phone number or person is really hard to remember when you are pregnant, but information that you've had stored for a while is relatively accessible. Kim used to forget why she left the house and it took some real focus and a look at her electronic calendar to figure out where she was supposed to be. Caitlin's memory was pretty much shot for three years after having the twins, so to help her work better she started to take notes on what she agreed to or discussed. At one point she even carried a digital recorder. So if people start saying things like "I already told you I was coming home late tonight" or "But you said that I had another week to finish the report," believe them. You might have developed the Teflon memory that accompanies baby brain. The good news is that the condition doesn't seem to last more than one or two years. Pregnancy brain can take quite a toll at work—the Australian scientists have also shown that multitasking is one of the first functions to be disrupted.

You may not realize your brain is changing, but there's no missing the big changes in your body. Gaining weight, even from a growing baby, can be stressful and depressing for pregnant women. When we lose confidence in our appearance, it's easy to lose confidence on other fronts too. Make looking good a priority—even when you're feeling poorly. Dress for success. By their nature, maternity clothes are a drag. They are style free, disposable and expensive, but don't fall into the muumuu trap. Be clever and resourceful. For example, low-rise jeans are a great option in the beginning, because they sit under the little bump. While researching this book, we found the BellaBand from Ingrid & Isabel (www.ingridandisabel .com) designed and marketed by mompreneur Ingrid Carney after she used a tube top around her waist to keep her jeans up. According to their Web site, the BellaBand will help you stay in your regular clothes through the postpartum period.

But you are going to need a few key new pieces for your working wardrobe. Be smart about your investment, though. A couple of great pieces (not shapeless shifts), supplemented with inexpensive T-shirts and yoga pants, will go a long way. Kim survived her entire pregnancy on three form-fitting Liz Lange cashmere sweaters and three pairs of Liz Lange black pants in escalating sizes. She found trousers a better option because they could camouflage the sensible shoes that she had to wear, both for safety and ever-swelling ankles. Since Kim's pregnancy, Liz Lange has launched a great-looking and value-priced line for Target. The clothes are stylish and inexpensive and hold up so you can pass them along to pregnant friends. If you work in an industry where five-hundred-dollar suits are the norm, check out www.babystyle.com for some more expensive but quality pieces.

when bad things happen to good women

The prevailing wisdom is that getting and staying pregnant is the easiest thing in the world. Unfortunately the reality is quite different. According to the American Pregnancy Association, 33 percent of American women lose their pregnancies, and as of 2005 more than 12 percent of American women of childbearing age have undergone fertility treatment of some kind. These are not small numbers, and the longer you wait, the harder it often is. So take care, girls, you could be in for a rough road as these two stories (both with happy endings!) illustrate. We share these stories as a reminder that things don't (and won't) always go as planned, but you can see from these experiences that a positive attitude, clear-headedness, and flexibility will help you navigate even the toughest waters.

the word

WHAT DOESN'T KILL YOU MAKES YOU STRONGER

Even before she was married, Katie Wainwright knew she would have fertility problems. At thirty-three, she got married and went straight to the fertility clinic at Cornell Medical Center in New York City. After reviewing her history, the doctors skipped over all of the less-invasive fertility options and went straight to IVF. In vitro fertilization is no picnic. When all other methods of assisted reproduction have failed (drugs, insemination, etc.), doctors resort to in vitro fertilization, or IVF. Simply put, a woman is given hormones by injection to stimulate egg production. Her hormone levels are monitored daily and when they hit the right level, the eggs are retrieved from the ovaries. Doctors will then fertilize them in a lab and monitor which ones look the most viable. Two to five of the most viable eggs are implanted in the woman's uterus with hopes one or more will attach and grow into a healthy fetus. It's painful and time consuming.

For Katie, IVF meant that every morning she left her West Village apartment at 6:30 a.m. and traveled to the Upper East Side of Manhattan to get to the hospital by 7:30 a.m. to get on the list for blood work so she could make it across town and be at her desk by 9:00 a.m. It should be noted that there were never fewer than one-hundred women at the hospital waiting for their blood work with her. And every evening she and her husband had to be home by 6:30 p.m. to administer her daily and painful shot of hormones. She wasn't telling anyone at work that she was going through fertility treatments, so getting to work on time was her number one priority. But it was by no means easy. The hormones made her feel crazy and stressed, and she was desperate for it to work. And luckily it did. She got pregnant with her first child on the first try.

Then something went wrong. She had a bad reaction or a side effect (they never determined which) to the IVF and she became "hyper stimulated" from the hormones. She blew up (literally, she started retaining fluid) and ended up in the hospital for forty-eight hours and out of work for ten days. This is a dangerous condition and, although she was out of danger, she looked five months' pregnant in her third week.

She told everyone at work that she had an allergic reaction to some medication and after ten days went back to work as if nothing had happened. (It's important to note that Katie had a stressful job at the time, running a publicity department for a major publisher—you didn't just drop out of work for ten days in her kind of job.)

She kept her pregnancy a secret for three months, except for the one colleague she had to tell because she was traveling on business and needed someone she could trust to administer her hormone shot (even after she was pregnant she continued to get the hormone shots).

Her first son, Jack, was born two weeks late after an emergency C-section. All in all, after the fertility treatments, a severe bout of carpal tunnel from the pregnancy, and the emergency surgery,

Katie had a healthy baby boy. After twelve weeks, she went back to work in great form. Her management welcomed her back and, although there was a bit of a tough transition because of the stress she had been under, she was back to 100 percent within a couple of weeks. She even earned a promotion to associate publisher. Things at work were operating very well. Her department was successful and her boss had promised her increased responsibilities and new challenges.

Katie and her husband had always wanted two children, and so when Jack was a little over a year old they started the IVF process again. After thirteen months and four failed attempts, Katie was despondent. During the fourth retrieval, the doctors found a polyp, which can form when you have too many fertility treatments. They removed it surgically and Katie needed a month to recover before she could try again.

She was still keeping her secret, but it was taking a toll on her personally and professionally. Two weeks after an implantation, she would call from work for the result, only to hear yet again that she wasn't pregnant. Every time the IVF failed, she'd go through a hormone crash. As much as her mind (and body) wasn't on the job, Katie poured herself into work for two important reasons. First, she needed something to go well in her life and, second, she had exhausted her insurance and was using her savings to pay for the treatments at $7,000 a pop. She literally couldn't afford to lose her job.

After the third failed attempt, Katie told her boss what was going on. She was still doing her job, but was distracted and felt obligated to share the news. While her boss was personally sympathetic, she made it clear that it was Katie's problem and had better not impact her work.

On her sixth and final IVF (any more were just too dangerous), Katie got pregnant. She was panicked about the possibility of miscarriage; however, she had to tell her boss early in her pregnancy because they were going to a trade show where she couldn't do any heavy lifting. Her pregnancy proceeded as normal for the next few weeks and she was back to work in full form.

At her thirtieth week sonogram, everything looked great. Three days later she was spotting and headed to the hospital for monitoring. The baby's heartbeat was dipping slightly, so they admitted her for observation. She was worried about missing any more work time because she had been so distracted and wanted to go out on maternity leave with everything in good shape. And then six doctors rushed into her room because the baby was in distress. They moved her into a private room, put her on an IV to try and develop the baby's lungs with medication, and sent a team down from the neonatal intensive care unit (NICU) to explain the realities of a baby born at thirty weeks.

She heard what they were saying but didn't believe it. She had to get back to work. She wasn't delivering a baby that day. And then she felt a gush of liquid, which turned out to be blood, and by 1:00 p.m. on September 28, fifty-five days early and less than four hours after she had gotten to the hospital, she was rushed into emergency surgery and delivered a very sick 2.8-pound baby girl.

Her husband called her boss and her NICU marathon began. After a couple of weeks of pumping, staying with her baby all day, and going home to her son at night, Katie asked if she could come back to work part-time right away so that she could save some maternity leave to use when her baby came home from the NICU. But she learned that, by law, mothers have to take maternity leave right at birth, so she had no choice and was offered no alternative options by her employer. Her boss made it clear that she wasn't wanted back unless she could come back full-time. When she did go back to work full-time after her tiny daughter came home from the hospital, she realized that her working environment had changed and that her boss seemed to have residual resentment about Katie's time off that affected their working relationship. Fortunately, three months later a dream opportunity presented itself and she left for a different company.

We asked her why she didn't just give up working for a while and stay home with her babies and her answer struck a note with us: "Before I came back from having Lucy, I loved my job. I like working and I am not cut out to be just at home doing the child care thing. Plus, we need the income. My children are well-rounded and have a wonderful life. I love having a career, and I have worked for eighteen years. I did not realize how much stress I was under at the time, but I was fortunate that it all worked out for my career and my family. I remind myself now, what doesn't kill me will make me stronger. I love my new job, and even if it is easily three times more responsibility and stress than the one I left, my children are doing well, and I am no longer distracted. I am very lucky."

the word

ON THE JOB

Kara was a sportswriter for a national magazine married to another sportswriter and trying to start a family. She was about ten weeks' pregnant when she was assigned to cover a hockey tournament training camp in Columbus, Ohio. At the first practice, she sat in the stands and listened to a colleague talk about his newborn son. She kept quiet about her own baby news—as she was supposed to for another couple of weeks—and excused herself to use the ladies room.

At that time, she noticed a little spotting. It was not much and she wasn't even sure if she had seen correctly, so she went through the rest of her work at the arena for the next couple of hours and then returned to the hotel. Once there, she was sure and called her obstetrician, who told her not to panic, to drink a lot, put her feet up, relax, and wait to see what happened next. It could be nothing, the doctor told her. Try not to worry.

Easier said than done, but this is where work became a great escape. After researching the area hospitals to know exactly where she would go if needed, Kara did her best to put aside her situation and put work first.

She finished her current assignments, then started planning ahead. If something was going wrong, she needed to have her work set up so she didn't leave any loose ends. At the time, her managing editor was not her biggest fan. She was already worried he would see her pregnancy as vulnerability and seek to exploit it. If somehow the pregnancy left her unable to do her job for any period of time, for whatever reason, he would definitely use it to his advantage. She was not about to let that happen.

That night, Kara told one person at the office—a friend and colleague who also happened to be pregnant. She was involved with Kara's assignments, so now if something urgent happened and Kara somehow couldn't be contacted the next day without notice, somebody in the loop knew what was going on. They not only discussed the personal situation but Kara also updated her colleague on the progress of the stories for that week's magazine and the future plans for covering the tournament.

The next day, after many hours in the Ohio State University Medical Center emergency room confirming the miscarriage in progress, she returned to the hotel to pack and wait to leave for the airport. Again, she used organizing work as a way to think about something else—and let anyone and everyone know her job was important to her and she would do it in a professional and responsible manner no matter the situation.

First she filed the stories she had finished the night before. She then e-mailed the public relations staff of the local team to tell them she wouldn't need her press box seat for the next night's game. She would have to deal with these people again and professional consideration was in order no matter what her situation. Again, she did not share the details of her story. Many women need and want to tell their tale, but work colleagues are not the people with whom to share such serious and personal information. She sent an e-mail to her pregnant friend in the office with news of the miscarriage, as well as some organizational stuff about the next week's stories.

Kara did not want her news to get out to everyone in the office, in particular her editor, so she called the editorial director—the big boss—a couple of times on his cell phone (it was the weekend). He did not answer, so she left a message about a family emergency and left Columbus for home. (She would later tell him the truth and apologize—although not completely sincerely—for leaving the assignment without getting through to him first. It should be noted, he could not have been more supportive.)

Of course, there isn't always time to move down a professional checklist, and often such things are the last thing on your mind. But it's not unimportant and it has multiple purposes.

First, it can take your mind off whatever is happening—and seems to be happening in some kind of horrible, super-slow motion film reel.

Second, it shows that you value your work and your company.

Finally, you can return to work without anyone doubting your commitment or focus.

girl talk

PERFECTIONISTS AND PREGNANCY

Girl's Guide friend, publishing colleague, original member of our book group, former client, and now working mom Leigh Ann Ambrosi gave birth to a beautiful baby boy on February 20, 2008. As the vice president for marketing and publicity for Sterling Publishing, she manages a department of twenty and is responsible for nine direct reports.

Leigh Ann is one of those girls who makes you feel less together. Gorgeous, with a killer body that she maintains with a rigorous exercise schedule, Leigh Ann always looks like she's walked out of the pages of a catalog. In the ten years we've known her, she's never been one minute late and is as organized as they get. You want to hate her but can't. She's as kind as she is perfect—never forgets a birthday, shows up to every event to lend support, and is never more than a phone call away if you need her. She's also darn good at her job. Focused, driven, and goal-oriented, she became a vice president in her early thirties and is now in a senior leadership position at a growing company.

She and her husband live in Princeton betwixt her Manhattan and his Philly job—which gives her an hour-and-forty-five-minute commute. Before Max, she would get up every morning at 5:45, be at her desk by 8:30, work until 7:00, and get home just before 9:00. She hit the gym three nights a week and both days on the weekends. She attended at least one evening professional event per week, and she's never gone to bed with a dirty dish in the sink.

We spoke to Leigh Ann the day of Max's six-month checkup on her last summer Friday in 2008. We wanted to know how a perfectionist made a smooth transition from pregnancy to working motherhood.

So, how is it?
It's been a million times harder than I've ever expected, but the reward has been a million times greater than I expected too.

How do you mean?
You're going to laugh, but I saved Tina Constable's Maternity Leave Bible (Tina was a publisher at Random House and Leigh Ann's former boss and mentor) that she had given us when she went out on maternity leave. She did a great job preparing us for when she left, and I knew when I got pregnant I wanted to use this as a model.

That was ten years ago!
It was eight years ago. You know I am a planner. I like to be prepared.

How did that plan go?
Well, not exactly as I hoped. First, getting pregnant was neither smooth nor easy for us. I got pregnant, but it wasn't going great and I had to go to a number of doctor's appointments and started missing work. I was allowed to go to work, but then I had to go straight home and put my feet up. After a prior flawless attendance record, I was worried that my bosses would start to wonder about my absences, so I told them at six weeks I was pregnant. I miscarried that pregnancy in my tenth week. After two days at home, I wanted nothing more than to go back to work and be normal. No one on my staff knew and work went on as usual.

How was the next pregnancy?
Nine months later I got pregnant again. The doctors never found out what happened to the first one. It was just one of those things.

At the time I had no idea how common miscarriages were and I thought I was the only one, not one in three. So with this pregnancy, I was a nervous wreck. I was spotting in the beginning and they gave me an almost weekly ultrasound.

When and how did you share the news about this pregnancy?
I told my bosses at thirteen weeks. I could keep it hidden because I didn't have the attendance issues. I had to use my vacation days because they were running out and the appointments weren't every week. I wanted to wait until it was 100 percent okay. By thirteen weeks, I couldn't hide it anymore, I was starting to show. I told my staff individually. Everyone found out the same week and was thrilled for me. It really is a very family-friendly company. The members of the executive team are all young with young children at home and really want the work-balance equation to work for their employees.

How did things change at work when you were pregnant?
I still got to work on time every day, but other things had to give. Pregnant Leigh Ann was exhausted, barely making it home awake. I would be falling asleep at the dinner table. I was nauseous all the time. I'd get on the 7:20 a.m. train with a ginger ale and bag of saltines. I had to stop going to the gym during the week because I was just too tired!

Prior to my pregnancy, I used to go to every single evening author event, every corporate event, the awards dinners, you name it, anything publishing-wise, I was there to represent. That stopped. I wasn't in the mood. I didn't feel good. I was getting fat and just not feeling it. I started delegating more and it became a great opportunity for my staff to do the things that I was always doing. I'll admit it took a little while, but I was so tired that I had to prioritize. Sooner or later I'd have to let go and this was my time. I was lucky. My staff really stepped up.

How did you prepare for your maternity leave?
My brilliant plan was to leave two full weeks before my due date on March 4. My last day of work was going to be February 15 and then

I would go home and get everything ready. As I mentioned, I had Tina's handy maternity pack as my guide and in January I started working on my own. Every day I would make a note of everything that I had done, and when I had down time or during lunch, I would flesh out each entry, explaining how to do everything in detail. It ended up being a ten-page document. I gave a copy to all of the department heads, my bosses, and then each individual who was responsible for covering parts of my job. I had meetings with everyone, all my work was done, and they even threw me a baby shower on February 13. February 15 was my last day at work.

Why did you take two weeks off before your due date?
The commute was killing me and the doctor wanted me to take it easy. Also, I had planned to use the time to get everything ready: pack a bag, finish the baby's room, and try to remove myself from my work routine so I could prepare for the new mother thing. Five days later my water broke. My maternity leave officially began on February 20, 2008. So much for my two weeks off...I had two *days!*

What is the company maternity policy and what did you do?
From the date your doctor pulled you out of work, the company pays in full until your due date. After that, you have six weeks of full pay for a vaginal delivery and eight weeks full pay for a cesarean. My goal was to be gone from work for twelve to fourteen weeks, I was going to use some vacation time and take two weeks unpaid.

you're a mommy now

Your little baby or babies are home from the hospital and you and she and your partner are trying to figure each other out. Does *that* cry mean I'm hungry or I'm tired? Is *that* cry belly pain? Is the baby latched onto the breast properly? Is it supposed to hurt? Am I supposed to be this tired? Doesn't this baby ever sleep somewhere other than my chest? Why can't his father calm him down? Why doesn't his father know where the extra wipes are? Why am I still fat?

Your career girl life as you knew it is completely forgotten. In those first few days, it's almost as if it never existed. Your maternity leave has begun in earnest and all those grandiose visions of resting and recuperating while the baby is sleeping have disappeared. This mommy thing is hard work and your maternity leave may be the only uninterrupted time you have with your child, so make the most of every moment.

Even if you are lucky enough to have help—an experienced relative, doula, or baby nurse—you are still trying to figure it all out. You are the mother and two weeks ago considered yourself quite competent. How hard could mothering possibly be? Generations of other women have done it. Now you wonder, why can't you get your baby to sleep? Or eat? Or nurse?

Don't despair. Pretty soon you'll be a pro and your mind will start focusing on other concerns like what's happening at work. You may even worry: Are things running smoothly without me? More smoothly than when I was there? This chapter will arm you with the strategies you need to enjoy your maternity leave and reenter the workforce smoothly.

hey, superwoman! the first three months are hard. really hard.

Your friends will tell you. Your colleagues will tell you. Your mother will tell you. But there's really no telling you until you've lived through the first three months of motherhood. How hard can it be with nothing to do all day but take care of a baby? Up until this point you've been managing projects, people, crazy bosses, and busy partners and still finding a way to carve out time for yourself. Now you're feeding, changing, comforting, and, in between, napping, doing some laundry, and hanging out. There's no reason you can't check a few e-mails, join a few conference calls, and, if you have a flexible partner or child care lined up, venture out for a meeting or two. Right? Wrong.

Be realistic and be adaptable. The baby will not work on your schedule. As a matter of fact, you will be lucky to get into any schedule whatsoever if you are breast-feeding on demand. In the first few weeks, breast-feeding and/or pumping take over your life. Work is the last thing you will be thinking about or able to focus on if some-one should call with a question. Plan for complete radio silence from work for at least three weeks. Let your boss know you've deliv-ered, send a photo (not one of you in the hospital or the baby naked—nobody wants to see those), and set expectations and limits on your availability.

After your imposed three-week exile, if you want to become ac-cessible, make it a goal to check e-mail once a day or keep your BlackBerry by your side as Caitlin did. Instruct one person to call you and leave a message in an emergency. You will respond within twenty-four hours. Otherwise, you are on baby time now. And baby time is 24/7. Don't beat yourself up for not getting anything done at home or at work. And don't ever turn down an offer for help. If your mother-in-law, who drives you absolutely crazy, offers to come and watch the baby for a couple of hours a week, accept the offer and give yourself a couple of options on how to spend the time, excluding housework. Take a nap. Do some work. Get out of the house. Don't spend your precious couple of hours cleaning bottles and doing laundry. And be flexible: What sounded great two days ago might in fact not work at all today.

Does it suddenly seem that everyone you know has become a stay-at-home mom? Does it seem every time you turn on the televi-sion another celebrity mom has given birth and is already back to work in their size 0 jeans? Does it seem like you are the most disor-ganized, exhausted, fat new mother you've ever met? Did most things you did and thought before you gave birth seem a lifetime ago and completely irrelevant right now?

If you've answered yes to all of these questions, congratulations, you are now officially a new mother. Don't worry, these feelings too shall pass. But now is the time to review all of those plans you for-mulated during your pregnancy: personal, professional, and finan-cial.

how do you feel?

Your insides hurt. Your outsides hurt. Your uterus hurts. Your boobs hurt—if you're trying to breast-feed they are engorged and if you're not they are engorged. In short, everything hurts. We were prepared for our maternity leave, but we weren't prepared for the pain. It's no wonder you need time off. It's more than figuring out what to do with this new baby; your body has to recover.

According to the Kids Health Web site for parents (www.kids health.org) created by a grant from the Nemours Foundation, in the first few weeks postpartum you should expect sore breasts, constipation, an uncomfortable episiotomy, hemorrhoids, hot and cold flashes, urinary or fecal incontinence, "after pains" from uterine contractions, vaginal discharge, and of course you still feel enormous (celebrity moms' overnight transformations notwithstanding). Yikes.

"I was not prepared for how badly I felt physically," recalls Leigh Ann Ambrosi. "My episiotomy didn't heal correctly either, so I had to have two follow-up procedures in my seventh week postpartum. I expected to at least be curious about what was happening at work but, in the beginning, I was so tired and hurting that I didn't even give it a second thought."

But the pain is not limited to the physical; the same site reports that, "up to 80 percent of new moms experience irritability, sadness, crying, or anxiety, beginning within days or weeks postpartum. These 'baby blues' are very common and may be related to physical changes (including hormonal changes, exhaustion, and unexpected birth experiences) and the emotional transition as you adjust to changing roles and your new baby."

If you've had a cesarean, it's even harder. You will hear people talk about their C-sections as if they had a tooth filled. Don't believe them. A C-section is major surgery and includes a painful recovery. There is a reason that mothers who have had C-sections are given two extra weeks of leave.

More serious than the baby blues, postpartum depression (PPD) occurs in 10–25 percent of new moms. Postpartum depression can cause mood swings, anxiety, guilt, and persistent sadness. In her book *Down Came the Rain: My Journey Through Post-Partum Depression*, Brooke Shields writes, "This was sadness of a shockingly different magnitude. It felt as if it would never go away." She shares how she denied anything was wrong and only because of the persistence of friends and her husband was she persuaded to seek treatment through medication and therapy. She also admits to having suicidal thoughts.

Researchers aren't totally sure what causes PPD, but they suspect that dropping hormones, along with environmental changes like exhaustion, being overwhelmed, and feelings of stress and loss of identity, can combine to set it off. The baby blues normally go away within a few days to a week. We didn't speak to one new mother who didn't break down in tears of frustration or exhaustion in the first weeks postpartum. Postpartum depression can happen anytime within the first year after childbirth and the symptoms are frighteningly similar to the baby blues. Keep track of the duration of the symptoms. Baby blues becomes postpartum depression when the feelings don't go away. If you or a loved one thinks you may be suffering from PPD, talk to your doctor as soon as possible.

evaluating your options

Now that you've been home with the baby a few days or weeks, you may be wondering if it's even realistic for you to go back to work. Is there ever going to be a child care situation that you will be comfortable with? Can you afford going back or staying home? Are you even the stay-at-home type? There comes a point in everyone's maternity leave when you ask yourself, what if I don't go back? Now's the time to give that some real thought.

After reviewing your options, dollars and cents might actually make some decisions for you. Your income and benefits may be necessary. Child care is expensive, but so is not working. Track your monthly expenditures. How much do you need to earn to pay for the essentials? And do you really want to live on just the essentials? Be honest with yourself about the type of lifestyle you want. As our favorite working mother, Linda Malkin, a risk management executive at a major hospital always tells us, "A happy mother is a good mother."

If you are going to be miserable because you are living on a tighter budget, then that's probably not the best option for you. Remember, it's not an *all* or *nothing* proposition. You don't have to go straight back to work or give up work forever. Jennifer Heth, a working mom in Denver, says, "I haven't worked full-time since having kids. I worked for three years, part-time when Emma was little. After Charlie was born, I quit that job. I volunteered full-time (i.e., 40 hours/week) for about four years, but that certainly isn't the same as career-work. I am back at work again, but only three days a week. Working motherhood for me is definitely a balancing act."

If you work for yourself or are in a position where if you don't work, you don't get paid, then cherish the first couple of weeks at home because that may be the only down time you get.

But keep in mind throughout your maternity leave, if you continue to feel like it will be impossible to jump back into a forty-hour workweek, you *do* have options you can explore with your employer. Perhaps you can arrange a part-time schedule for a few weeks, or come in late and leave early. You certainly don't want to send a message that you aren't taking your return to work seriously, so be sure you set up a concrete schedule and a clear time frame with your employer.

Jayne Schmidt, a first-time mother of a six-month-old, works for the Council on Accreditation (www.coa.org). She wrote the standards for "Early Childcare and Development Services" for multi-social service providers, which are facilities that provide more than child care, such as community centers, so she knows a thing or two about child care. Jayne recommends slowly transitioning into child care and back to work, if at all possible. When a new babysitter first starts, Jayne works from home for about three days, observing and training. When she first went back to work, her employer allowed her to begin first with half-days, working her way back a little more each week until she was fully on the new schedule after a couple of months. She now works four eight-hour days. "Transitioning back into work over time really helped me both at home and at the office. I was able to give my full attention to wherever I was because I wasn't worrying about what was happening at the other place," she says.

when a girl's just gotta get back to work

If you are in a job where if you don't work you don't get paid, maternity leave is generally shorter or blurred. Whether you own the business or are an hourly-wage worker or work for a small company, your time is literally your money, maternity leave fits in when you can afford it. But planning will most definitely help.

If you are running a business with an infrastructure and a team, then you can set up a system that will cover for you while you are gone. When Chris Colabella, owner and president of Construction Information Systems in New Jersey, was pregnant with her first daughter in 1997, she was the vice president in charge of operations and had a staff of eighteen—most of whom were in operations. To cover her maternity leave, she broke her group into separate departments and assigned "team leaders" to each department who would oversee the work. It's a system that she still employs now. She was already removed from the daily tasks that needed to get done, so her presence wasn't needed day-to-day to keep the company running smoothly as long as her team leaders were in place.

Financially, though, it was a different picture. The company was small enough not to be covered under the FMLA act, and they offered no paid maternity leave—even for an owner—so after she had her baby, she went on short-term disability from the state. She chose to keep her paycheck coming and worked twelve days past her due date when she was finally induced. She stayed home for four weeks, stayed in touch, did a little work, and even stopped in a few times. To many this would sound pretty skimpy, but the benefit of owning your own business, even if you can't afford to leave it unattended, is that it offers what many women describe as the key factor to successful working motherhood: flexibility.

Chris shared her story with us:

I was so preoccupied with my first pregnancy with my daughter Kali that my work really suffered. I was aware of every single thing that was going on with my body. I was on a very strict diet. I made doctor appointments at very inconvenient times because I only wanted to see certain physicians in the practice. While at work, I was "researching" baby-related info on the Web and running out to visit day care centers and I was constantly worried about how I was going to balance it all because motherhood and my career were both a priority.

When I returned from my maternity leave with Kali, I set up an elaborate schedule to maximize my time with her. I worked four days per week, one of which I brought her into the office. Her father could telecommute (he worked for AT&T at the time) and took care of her at home twice a week and her grandmother watched her the fifth day. This went on for months but wasn't really working because of unexpected changes in all of our schedules. I finally put her into day care when she was seven months old for four days while she continued to go to her grandmother's for the fifth. Once she was in day care, I left work early to pick her up at 3:30 p.m. so I could spend the afternoons with her. I worked only 35 hours per week until Kali was one year old and did very little to further the growth or productivity of my company. At work I maintained the status quo. At home I was trying to be supermom—cooking, cleaning, and spending quality time with my daughter and husband.

I remember it as very hectic and horrible, with lots of running around and an added problem. Like most kids, Kali was getting sick at day care. I had to take time off or would try to work from home (near impossible with a sick child) or I just gave up and brought her to the office with me. (I tried not to think about how she would infect the other people.) She even contracted salmonella at day care—which was a disaster. She was out of school for an entire month, and although her grandmother helped, I missed even more work. Luckily by two years old she had built up a healthy immunity to those crazy day care germs and I was finally on a schedule! Shortly thereafter I got pregnant with my second daughter and started the whole thing over again. Because I had a system that I had perfected over two years, I just plugged my second daughter into it with a few important upgrades. When Myah started getting sick from day care, I pulled her out and hired a nanny. I couldn't afford to miss months of work this time as I had been promoted and taken on more responsibilities.

As I added more value to the company (funny what happens when you can actually devote yourself to work), my compensation increased too. I was able to outsource more of the household work that would fill up my weekends and cause me to miss time with my children. I took control of my calendar and continue to be very organized and scheduled. I guess I've never really seen the work/mother balance as a problem to solve at work, but rather one to solve at home by lining up child care, household help, and a group of supportive people to step in when needed. As a business owner I had many options that an employee of any kind wouldn't have. I had already built up my staff to do everything that needed to be done, whether it was accounting, operations, or sales. I just had to manage and oversee that process. My role at work was strategic development and my work decisions directly affected how we would grow our company. I weighed the options (work/mother balance again) and made a decision to grow more slowly. I also hired more people so that I didn't have any direct responsibility for the product or the sales, which continues to give me flexibility, and I've promoted people to be team leaders and managers so that I could be more autonomous. It's been a painfully slow and frustrating process, wasting a lot of time and money on incompetent people, but it's starting to come together now. I have a good staff, the company runs itself, I'm finally making decent money, I work only thirty-five to forty hours per week, and I never gave up the time with my kids.

who's taking care of the children?

This is the most important section in the book. For women to be successful at work they must have dependable child care. Period. Nanny or day care, stay-at-home dad or in-home situation, it makes no difference. Quality and reliability are what you're looking for, and finding quality child care will be your first major parenting challenge. You're looking for a mommy or daddy substitute—someone who will nurture, love, cuddle, play with, and care for your child when you're at work. And boy, do you need to plan ahead. In many cities across the country, reliable, affordable child care takes time to find. Competition for the best providers, whether it's a nanny or a day care center can be intense. And, of course, expensive.

Investigate all of your options before you make any decisions. When you're pregnant, you might be convinced you can't live without a nanny only to walk by a day care center and fall in love with the warm, supportive environment you observe. Child care options include day care centers, home day care, nanny care, preschool, relative care, and staying at home.

Not surprisingly, day care is best when teacher-to-child ratios are low. Look past the flashy set-ups. Pay special attention to how the caregivers interact with the children. Ask plenty of questions. And you can never start too early. It could take as long as six months to find an ideal situation for your budget. These women (child care providers are almost exclusively women) are going to be your surrogates during the day. You want them to treat your baby in the same manner you would. Day cares are regulated, too. Make sure you check out their accreditation. Only about six thousand centers have been accredited by the National Association for the Education of Young Children (NAEYC)—the highest standard around.

Jayne Schmidt recommends you do a lot of research in advance and come to each day care center armed with a list of questions for the administrator, teachers, and other parents you meet. She also recommends that you check the resources of your local community. For example, in Westchester County, N.Y., where she lives, the Childcare Council of Westchester provides a list of licensed child care providers in Westchester, as well as provides resources to help choose the right placement for your child.

Some things you should consider: What is the ratio of teachers to kids? How much time do the children spend outside? What is the curriculum? How often is the school closed for meetings and holidays? What is the teacher turnover? How much parental participation is expected? What are the hours? Are they fully licensed, inspected, and accredited? Are the kids actually learning or just playing? Are there art supplies, instruments, sports equipment, and/or computers?

We spoke to a number of women who put their children in "in-home" day care. The advantages they reported included proximity to their homes and small "class size" (including sometimes even one-on-one care), as well as the low cost compared to other options. References for in-home day care become crucial because so few of them are licensed or accredited.

If you've never done any hiring in your professional life, you might want to read a few books. Alicia Rockmore, entrepreneur and busy working mom, offers great advice a little later in this chapter. The goal when hiring a nanny is to find someone to care for your child with love, confidence, and professionalism and someone who respects your authority. You are the parent and set the rules. As with all good employees, a nanny should show up on time every day, leaving her personal issues at home. In addition to her professionalism, look for someone who will be loving and extremely vigilant with your child.

Before you start interviewing nannies, create a list of job expectations. Consider: What are your office hours? How long is your commute? How long do you need to get ready in the morning? How soon could you realistically get home after work? Are there ever unavoidable late nights at the office? Are you looking for child care only or do you need someone who will do housework when the children are napping? Set the parameters of the schedule and responsibilities, then review your budget. Additional time and responsibilities cost money. Can you afford a nanny who can stay late three nights a week or must you simply leave work to relieve her? Ask your neighbors, friends, and coworkers how much they pay their nannies. Rates and expectations vary from city to city.

If you're able to hire a good nanny, then you have more than an employee, you have a partner in your home, helping you teach and guide your children as well as taking care of the more mundane domestic issues: laundry, cooking, and cleaning. Unfortunately, you can become absolutely dependent on the nanny and because there is only one of them (unlike a day care center), if she gets sick or has personal issues that keep her at home, you are in trouble.

Caitlin went through four nannies (four!) before deciding to put the twins into a preschool (fancy name for day care center) at age two. The first nanny turned out to be a racist. The second was excellent but was with them for only a year because she decided to do missionary work in South America. The third nanny was unprofessional and heartless—after four months with the twins, she didn't even take a moment to call over a weekend after Caitlin's son had surgery on Friday. Later they were told by a neighbor that this same nanny would leave the kids strapped in a stroller while she made cell phone calls in the courtyard. The fourth nanny, although highly recommended, showed up late almost every day, would often call in sick, and, here's the kicker, was caught drinking sweet vermouth when babysitting late one night.

So, after the Friedmans' string of really bad luck with the nanny train, they decided to enroll the twins into what would be an excellent preschool around the corner.

What Caitlin learned about having a nanny care for your children is that she really needed someone who would show up on time every day. She needed someone who cared for and about the kids. She needed someone who was open-minded, energetic, and didn't drink (obviously!). The day care (preschool, nursery) around the corner provided all of that with its three teachers. And although slightly more expensive than a nanny because two kids are enrolled, it's worth every penny knowing that the school doors would be open at 8 a.m. and not shuttered because of migraine headaches.

If you have a relative willing to take care of your child for free, you may have hit the jackpot. But it's a difficult situation even if it seems like a dream come true. Even though it's a family member, you must treat it as a professional transaction. Be very clear about the work hours and your expectations for care. If your aunt is watching your baby and sticking her in front of the television for much of the day, you need to address it. If your mother offers to help out a few days each week, but you know that she can't get anywhere before 10 a.m., before accepting her generous offer, be very clear about your expectations.

As a working mom you need to line up help that actually helps you. Amanda Dantico, a young woman we spoke to who was raised by a working mother, advises us to "find a child care system that everyone is happy with," ideally "one that is flexible supported by friends and family." A good child care system makes it easier for you to get to work with a clear head and relatively guilt-free. If the people or the circumstances are making it difficult for you to get back into work mode, then you may need to make some changes.

Galia Gichon, a personal financial planner and author of *My Money Matters*, recommends that when thinking about child care you always overestimate the cost. She says, "If you think you are getting a financial deal, it most likely will not work out. As a working parent, you need reliable child care and that costs more than you think it will."

the word

Susan Stein is a mom and the director of a preschool, The Children's Garden, in Manhattan. We spoke to her about working mother guilt, how to work best with your day care teachers, and things to consider when you are interviewing schools:

We all know that dropping kids off at preschool is heartbreaking for the working mom. What would you like them to know to help them deal with their guilt or concerns about having other people take care of their children?

It's hard to describe just how seriously the teachers in our school take their job to care for the children in their charge during the day. Just about every one of our teachers is a working parent of necessity and has had to miss some occasion important to their child because of work commitments. They truly understand how difficult it is to leave their young child with someone else for long periods of the day, and they appreciate it when parents confide their own anxieties about child care to them. The teachers really do want to "fill in the blanks" of what goes on during the day or make a phone call to a parent to reassure them that their child is not merely being attended to, but that the teacher is really seeing their child. It goes a long way toward creating a relationship between the parents and teachers, which is absolutely essential to the child making a great adjustment to school. What I never fail to be amazed by and I would want every mother (and father) to know is just how quickly the teachers come to know and love each child in their class and how quickly the children ease into the classroom routines and bond with the teachers. How do I know this? When I walk into a class sometimes it's the teachers, other times it's the children, but there is always someone ready to share an anecdote about the day. They can be funny stories, sometimes they're triumphs, and sometimes they're describing a disappointment, but there's never any mistaking the pride on the teachers' faces or the smiles on the children, and there are infinitely many more smiles during a typical day than there are tears.

What should parents look for when interviewing preschools?

There is a definite intangible quality to the preschool visit, a certain gut feeling that yes, I see my child here, or no, I definitely don't. But there are a few things parents might also look for. What is the overall tone of the school? Do the teachers greet you if you come into their classroom and then move back to the children? Look at the children and their interactions with each other and the teachers.

Are they smiling, laughing, and maybe even singing? Do the teachers and children appear to be relaxed as they move around the classroom? Depending upon the age of the children, are the teachers at the level of the children engaged in the children's activities or in conversation with them, or are they standing above the children, talking to one another. If a child is crying or children are squabbling, are you comfortable with how the teachers handle the situation? Regarding the art work, does it appear to be done by young children, who have their own varying abilities and ideas, or can you see the hand of a teacher in the end product? Do the teachers use a variety of materials and can you get a sense of some of the things they've been exploring in the class? Are there areas for sand and water; a semblance of privacy, lots of books, a touch of nature? For lack of a better way to say it, is there anything cozy about the classroom that a young child can respond to or is everything exceedingly neat and precise? Are there things around the classroom that reflect the touch of the young children that spend a significant amount of time there, such as labeled family photographs, classroom photographs, birthday charts, cubby tags, etc. And of course, the subject that many prospective families mention to me: the importance of cleanliness. Things don't have to be in obsessive order, but the room, the toys, the general ambience should be one of cleanliness and good repair.

You were a working mom and you are the head of a preschool, so tell us how new working moms can best work with preschool teachers?

Once your child has become comfortable with the classroom routines at the beginning of the day, please come on time and greet the teachers. Model to your children that you are comfortable with the idea that they will be spending the day with them. Settle your child in, give a kiss or hug good-bye, and leave promptly so your child can make the transition to the school day. Please do not say, "I wish I could stay here and do nothing but play all day." Believe me, that does not endear a parent to very dedicated and hard-working teachers. Let the teachers know if there is anything unique to your child that will comfort him or her if need be. Make sure your contact numbers are up-to-date. Have a backup plan in the event your child gets sick, which you have to expect will happen. Teachers are uncomfortable turning sick children away and appreciate not being put on the spot. Try not to have your child be the last child to be picked up every evening. After a while, your child will notice it. From time to time incidents may crop up that will require you to meet with the teachers. Try to relax and remember that everyone in school really does have the best interests of your child at heart and just wants to make it as good as it can be for him or her. At the same time, though, remember, you are and will always be your child's best advocate, and misunderstandings between parents and teachers have been known to happen. If there's something you feel the teachers are missing or you want them to know, you must speak up and they will appreciate your candor.

Any suggestions for new moms who are preparing to put their children into preschool?
The one practical thing that immediately comes to mind is having your child on a schedule so that they come to school on time and rested, ready to have a great day. In addition, recognize that you and the teachers, through your interactions, will be working together to create a warm and loving environment that will nurture and sustain your child during the day and at the same time enable him or her to have a great time making new friends and learning new things.

THE UNEXPECTED

Kim loved every second of her pregnancy. Other than being a little tired in the first trimester, she felt fantastic. She worked for herself from home before she partnered with Caitlin and had only a few clients. She became obsessed with natural childbirth and took Bradley classes. Soon this Jersey girl started sounding like an earth mother from Berkeley. She wanted a drug-free birth and to be monitored as little as possible. She switched from an intervention-happy OB practice to a midwife in her seventh month. Four days before her due date, on December 30, 1999, she went into labor—although she didn't realize it until the next morning, when those pains weren't stopping. Her son Thomas was born at 10:40 on the morning of December 31, 1999, at a hospital in Teaneck, N.J.

It seemed to go well. Thomas popped out looking healthy except for what his parents likened to a big, red grape stuck on the front of his eye. The midwife didn't appear worried, but they took Thomas off for some more tests. Apparently, there was something wrong with both of his eyes. The doctors couldn't be sure, but it looked to them like Thomas was blind. Blind?! How did that happen? Why hadn't anyone seen it on the sonogram? What was going on? Thomas was whisked off in an ambulance with his father to the Neonatal Intensive Care Unit at Columbia Presbyterian Hospital in New York City. They didn't know how to treat him in Teaneck. As one of the nurses told Kim after he was born, "We don't get babies like that here." So six hours later, Kim signed herself out and was on her way across the river to be with her son.

Why are we telling this story? Kim was self-employed and her husband had just quit his job to take care of the baby while she worked. In short, if she didn't work, she didn't get paid. But who could think about work when she had a blind child? On the other hand, if she didn't work, how was she going to take care of the blind child?

The good news is that after a couple weeks of testing, some crazy scares, and a lot of intense observation, Kim and her family learned Thomas was not fully blind. He is legally blind and categorized as visually impaired, but he's doing fantastically well in a mainstream public school.

Kim and her husband had prepared for maternity leave. She had told all of her clients she'd be taking two weeks off (which was great timing because of the holidays) and would be back to work the second week in January—except for one project that was due on January 5. She signed up for New Jersey's short-term disability insurance and had work lined up for the next three months.

And so in between trips to specialists (including an oncologist, who had to rule out that Thomas had retinoblastoma, a life-threatening cancer of the eye) and surgeons (Thomas had his first surgery at seven days old and his second at six months), Kim worked. She didn't have a choice and it probably saved her from losing her mind. Of course, she can't remember anything she worked on during that time, except for that one that was due on January 5. She still has perfect recall of every doctor visit with Thomas. But the point is, she made it through, with her business and sanity intact. She got extensions on most of the projects and has been blessed with a large and supportive family on both sides nearby.

Thomas's unexpected disability taught Kim a few important things that are worth passing along:

- Ask for help. Your friends and family (and in Kim's case, clients) will step up and be there for you. Her team of helpers were running errands, bringing food, changing diapers, and even editing press releases. Thomas's little village was born on the last day of the millennium, too.
- You can't plan for everything. When bad stuff happens, you'll just deal with it. Work may not be the priority at the moment of crisis, but as Kim's story illustrates, you can't just walk away from it either. Do the best you can. Be up front about what's happening and make every effort to get help.
- Stop trying to be perfect. We've noticed successful career women share some common traits and one of them is always striving for perfection. Prior to Thomas, Kim would spend two days laboring over writing a press release. After Thomas, she could suddenly knock one out in two hours. The end product wasn't much different— she just didn't have the time to strive for perfection anymore. As it turned out, good was more than good enough and, the funny thing is, it still is.

"ALICIA'S GUIDE TO HIRING AND KEEPING GREAT NANNIES"

Alicia Rockmore, the founder of Buttoned Up! (www.getbuttoned up.com), calls herself an organizational maniac and she seamlessly juggles a fast-paced career and full home life. Prior to co-founding Buttoned Up, Inc., Alicia was a marketing executive at Unilever. Alicia was a career girl and had no plans to quit working once her daughter was born. She has an MBA from the University of Michigan and is a CPA, too. But she knew even before her daughter Lucy came unexpectedly into the world at thirty-two weeks that she was going to need more flexibility in her job. She was willing to put in the hours but needed to be able to do them on her own schedule.

When she started looking for a new job, she realized that most of corporate America operated the same as Unilever—lots of travel, zero flexibility, and minimal control over your options for growth. At that point, she decided to start her own business and conceived and launched Buttoned Up!

She now works more than she has ever before and maintains that the key to her success as a happy working mother has always been a great nanny. Because she's moved a number of times, Alicia is an expert at interviewing nannies. She's hired nannies in New York City, Nashville, Tennessee, and Ann Arbor, Michigan. We spoke to her in mid-interview process in Los Angeles, California. Here are some of her techniques:

1. Excellent nannies are hard to find. Expect to pay them well and treat them as part of the family.
2. I interview nannies the same way I would for any other job. In Los Angeles, I called three agencies and had them send over ten candidates each. I can usually tell within five minutes which ones I want to interview further, because at first I have to like them. Then I ask

them questions that get to their instincts. "If you can't reach me and Lucy falls on the playground, what are you going to do?" I explain the job requirements and once I narrow down the list, say from thirty to three, Lucy becomes part of the process, too. I invite her to meet them and then watch how they interact with her. When she was a baby I had to rely on their work history and references.

3. When looking at work history and references, I always look for consistency. I want to see long placements in homes because that ultimately says more than a reference. The two best nannies I've ever had worked with their last families for more than ten years.

4. I prefer nannies who have no other obligations in their life. No kids, no husband or boyfriend. They are usually older. The hours are very flexible but generally from 7:00 a.m. to 6:00 p.m. They have to be willing to stay overnight even though my husband and I try not to travel at the same time.

5. And when you've got a good nanny, don't be afraid to give over tasks that it feels like a mom should do. When Lucy was a baby the nanny took her to music class and now the nanny packs Lucy's lunch. I choose to spend quality time with her and not do the routine stuff.

i'm back

Here's the thing, girls . . . you are different after you have a baby, and we aren't just talking about the obvious. You likely won't even realize all the ways you've changed until you've gotten back into your old routine.

You might find that you're anxious to go to work in the morning but, once at your desk, you want nothing more than to go home. Or, you might be downright furious that your beloved suits no longer look right. Maybe you find yourself reluctant to take on any new work, fearing you won't have the energy to get it done.

The reality is that you are a different kind of career woman now. You have huge new responsibilities and someone at home who doesn't care if you have a presentation the next morning. Your energy level, body, attention span, and focus are most likely not as they were before you had the baby. Our boy Jim wrote us to say, "The parent/child connection is the only one that can *never* be changed. Marriages, jobs, houses, they can come and go but you will always be a parent of that child. So don't pretend you can do it all—draw up new rules and boundaries and don't just hope it will all get back to normal."

Things have radically changed. It does not have to be a negative, it is just the reality. Life is now different, not necessarily better or worse. Once you realize that—and how you have changed—we recommend you embrace it.

will stella ever get her groove back?

For everyone who is at the beginning stages of pregnancy or for whom it is something they have envisioned for their future, it is common to idealize the baby phase—never imagining that the baby just won't go to sleep at 8:00 all of the time, even if you have a presentation to write that night. And no, the baby won't respect your meeting-packed schedule enough not to get sick on a Tuesday. And even if the future dad is nurturing and dependable and insists he will do 50 percent of the child care before you give birth, well, often it just doesn't work out that way. The fact is, being a completely honest and realistic—not bitter—working mom is profoundly difficult. You have not just the needs of your significant other, boss, coworkers, and family to consider; now you have an infant. And your baby needs more from you than all of the above combined.

Before jumping into the solutions, tips, and stories that will help you navigate this sometimes trying journey to get back into the work groove, we want you to know you are not alone. It isn't your imagination. Working motherhood is challenging. Even if you love being a mother and struggled to make it happen, even if you wanted it your whole life. You are still you, with dreams and ambitions, and setting those aside because of exhaustion or new responsibilities is difficult. It is also shocking to many of us who, during those first few weeks back at work, find ourselves surprisingly happy to be cranking out expense reports and worrying about what to order for lunch rather than being home unable to take a shower. That's normal and please don't beat yourself up. You love your baby, you love your home, you may also love your work. That's OK.

The biggest surprise to us is just how much of a toll the lack of sleep takes. Caitlin went back to work six weeks after her twins were born. And looking back on that foggy first three weeks back, when all she wanted to do was curl up and sob under her desk (and she is *not* a crier), she can't believe she made it through. Yes, she had a supportive business partner, and a helpful spouse, but still, after six weeks of being woken up every three hours, it was tough, really tough, to get back into the swing of things. So know that, again, it isn't just you. The toll that pregnancy takes on your body and hormones is significant, but also, caring for an infant is infinitely more exhausting than anything you have ever or will ever do. So be realistic about how much to take on when you get back to work.

Here we're going to show you ways to work smarter not just harder and help you get your (back to work) groove back.

am i ruining my child?

The first question you'll probably ask yourself on your first day leaving your child is, "Am I ruining her?" Of course you're not ruining her. Have you, to the best of your ability set up safe and reliable child care? Do you trust that in your absence your child's needs will be met? If you've answered yes to these questions, then without a doubt, you are absolutely not ruining your child by continuing to work. Read the studies. Children who are raised by people other than their parents have statistically the same chance of success as children who were raised by their parents.

The facts support working moms. The problem arises when all the facts in the world can't make your feelings of guilt go away. All you can do is make decisions that are right for you and your family based on needs, wants, goals, and financial realities. If you are miserable working then you need to find a way to make a change, but if you're not miserable working then you should focus on the positives. We spoke to several people who were raised by a working mom. When asked how they felt about their mother working, almost everyone said they appreciated having such an inspirational role model.

Several responded that they learned "independence" and "self-reliance" at an early age, which helped instill confidence. Sharon Lowenheim shared this: "I continued the same career for the first eight years of my post-motherhood life. I felt that it was important for my daughter to see that women worked, and that they could even be the primary bread-winner in their families (as I always was, even though my husband is a scientist)."

supermom doesn't exist (even in comics)

After coming to terms with the fact that you are not ruining your child, the second most important thing you're going to have to realize is that you can't do it all at work and at home. Period. There is no supermom. In the post-feminist seventies, all working moms are supposed to aspire to this icon. Now that we won the right to be at work, you can bring home the bacon, fry it up in a pan, bathe and feed the baby, and never let your husband forget he's a man. The freedom to be everything somehow became the responsibility of doing everything. Because the only way you can be a supermom or super career girl—keeping everyone fed, loved, and taken care of—is if you put yourself last. Maybe it can be done. But why would you want to and who would benefit from you killing yourself every day? Completely and totally neglecting yourself leads to burnout, nothing to give a partner, and little to no energy for your baby. And think it through a little bit: If you continued to put yourself last, your dreams, goals, and professional aspirations on the back burner, where will you be in eighteen years? Working while raising children isn't for everyone, but for those of us who consider work an integral part of who they are, we just can't afford to chase some supermom ideal. So start by giving it up. Accept that you can do it all, just not all at the same time. Remind yourself that keeping *you* in the mix helps everyone in the long run, and if your career is still a priority after having your baby, it is worth fighting for. With that said, you're mentally armed to be "back."

five ways to say . . . i'm back!

If you love your job it is essential to get those first few days, weeks, and months back at the office after maternity leave right. It isn't easy. Your hormones are still completely off, you may be breastfeeding, conflicted feelings about leaving your infant rise almost on the hour, and you may feel a little paranoid about your job security. In part, you are right to feel paranoid because even if your job isn't at stake, your reputation as a valuable asset to the company just might be. It's difficult to feel completely confident that you can make the successful return after seeing coworkers throw in the career towel after having kids. So take a deep breath and vow to take control of this reentry into work. Below we have outlined five actions to take within the first few months of your return that will shout out to your team and your boss . . . *I am back!*

MEET WITH THE BOSS

Schedule a meeting with your boss on your first day back. Go into this crucial get-together projecting enthusiasm for returning to work even if you are conflicted about it. If you need to, fake your energy and positive attitude, because this is business. Even if you are friendly with your boss, she is absolutely not your friend in this context. She may be happy for you, but she does not want you crying in the office about missing your baby. Often bosses have prepared themselves for you giving your notice or, at the very least, having lost your edge. If your job and career at this particular company are important to you, then you must prove them wrong. Be engaged, ask questions, demonstrate that you are up to speed, and, if possible, have even moved a few things forward. Bring up the meetings you have scheduled with your team to review current issues or projects. Spend as little time as possible talking about the personal aspects of your maternity leave. Instead take the opportunity to bring up things you read or watched that are relevant to your company. Your boss wants nothing more than to take worrying about you and your workload off her plate, so do it for her. And do it fast.

MEET WITH THE TEAM

If you have an assistant, a team, or an entire division, focus on managing the minute you are back behind your desk. Pull in your senior team members individually to express your appreciation for what they accomplished in your absence. Get down to business by asking to be filled in on everything they may not have told you during your leave. If people have been dropping the ball or trying to undermine you, chances are you heard about it from someone when you were gone. Confront the coworkers and the issues head on as soon as possible. It will show the team that you are strong and you are back if you nip problems in the bud.

GET OUT THERE

Unfortunately, people are going to assume that you are less relevant professionally now. Professional validation helps combat the invisibility issue many new mothers experience at work. So make it a priority, if you haven't already, to join high-profile groups and professional organizations. Don't go overboard with the commitments; you do have a baby and about a million other things to worry about, but because most professional organizations cater to working people, the events are often at breakfast or lunch. Be strategic about what you take on; you are looking for high visibility and an opportunity to share what you've done or learned with your team.

DRESS TO KILL

This is shallow (and more than a little bit annoying to many of us), but the truth is, we are often judged on our appearance. This especially holds true for the working mother. Many corporate cultures make it difficult for us to be heard, make an impact, and be respected as a peer. It doesn't seem fair that we are combating the assumptions that we would rather be home by taking on more than our colleagues, but that's often what we have to do, at least in the beginning. So, yes, it makes a difference if we return to work looking put together. How you present yourself says something to the outside world and, right now, you want to say . . . I'm back, so listen to me, respect me, and appreciate what I bring to this organization.

BE CONFIDENT

How you carry yourself those early days back at the office will set the tone for how you will be perceived moving forward. Contribute to the first team meeting by expressing your pleasure at being back. Don't be apologetic or tentative in any of those first meetings. You have no reason to be sorry. Maternity leave is your right and having a baby is your privilege, and don't let anyone make you feel bad about taking time away from the office. Project to your boss, colleagues, and staff that you belong back at the conference table.

building a rapport with your boss

When you get back from maternity leave, it might take a little while to reconnect with your boss. You've been out for a while and work has been moving along without you. She or he may also be experiencing some unconscious and conscious emotional reactions related to your return, including resentment you were gone, anxiety you will quit, concern that you have changed into another type of employee. You also want to remember that if you are having difficulties balancing everything, keep the personal stuff to yourself, as working mom Felicia Watson does: "If I'm going to miss a deadline (which almost never happens), I don't use my family or children as an excuse." Believe us, even if a sick child is the reason for being late on a project, don't bring that into it.

Here are some suggestions for how to build rapport with your boss:

MAKE HER JOB EASIER

That's really why you were hired. A boss manages people who work on projects or aspects of the business she is responsible for. Your role as her employee is to make that go more smoothly. While you were out, her job was made a little more difficult. Now that you've returned, take back the work that was left on her plate and start making it known that you are back to make her life easier.

SHARE YOUR BOSS'S CONCERNS AND PRIORITIES

Along the lines of "mirroring," where you are adopting the behavior of someone else in order to bond, we suggest that you tune into where your boss is coming from. If she is concerned about declining sales figures, then you outline how you are going to contribute to fixing the problem. You will have opportunities to bond with your boss if your actions and deliverables reflect her priorities.

SHOW YOU CARE

Demonstrate you are invested in your job, the team, and the company by being engaged in meetings, offering suggestions and solutions, asking questions, and taking on new responsibilities.

WORK HARD BUT WORK SMART

Since working moms have less time than they did before, you need to work just as hard but much more wisely. Efficiency and organization are the keys to finding that elusive work/life balance. Working harder but smarter will also appeal to your boss, who most likely could do without the long lunches and random office chats.

KNOW THE BOSS IS NOT YOUR FRIEND

When you find yourself talking to your boss, don't waste her time by chatting about the baby. Yes, a good friend cares about your personal life and wants to hear details, but a good boss often doesn't. You also don't know how what you're sharing is being interpreted. The story you told her about your son smiling for the first time could be heard as a hint that you are going to quit to be a stay-at-home mom. So keep it all to yourself and focus the conversations on work.

MEET REGULARLY

It is especially important in the first few weeks back to meet with your boss regularly. It's your chance to show him you are back in the swing of things. Be smart about what you discuss in the meetings and steer clear of sharing gossip or petty office issues.

Take opportunities to sell your accomplishments. In general, women don't do this enough, so much so that we dedicated huge sections in our *Kicking Your Career into Gear* book to the subject. It is most crucial for women just back from maternity leave to sell themselves, because we are often facing inherent sexism, including the assumptions that we should—or would—rather be at home.

notes on breast-feeding from lovers and haters

One of the biggest challenges you may have as a mom is breast-feeding. When Nicole Lamborne, an obstetrician/gynecologist and mother of three told us that they didn't teach her how to breast-feed in medical school, we weren't surprised. The prevailing wisdom is that breast-feeding is the most natural thing in the world (why would anyone have to teach you?)—your baby pops out, latches onto the breast, and you're off to the races.

The reality is that breast-feeding is difficult, at least in the beginning and it's especially difficult for working mothers because they have to pump. And pumping stinks (we're allowed to say that)—you have no connection to the baby, the machine is loud, there's nothing relaxing about sitting with your top down with two plastic bugles attached to your nipples sucking away. We haven't spoken to a mother yet, working or not, who enjoys expressing breast milk.

We represent both ends of the spectrum of the breast-feeding experience. Kim delivered Thomas at term, and although he couldn't see, he managed to find the breast and latch on. Because he was only in the NICU a couple of days, and able to nurse, she had to pump only a couple of times per day. When she got home from the hospital, with the help of a *Boppy* pillow, inconceivable amounts of water, and her husband, who kept pushing the baby's head in place, Kim was able to get into a groove. Since she worked from home for the first nine months, breast-feeding became an easy part of her routine after the second month. She had also purchased the Medela Pump n Style® like most new mothers do, thinking that she'd be popping that out between errands to pump like those new mothers you see in the breast pump advertisements. Ha! After the sterilizing and two hours of reading directions, she gave the pump away and supplemented occasionally with formula.

Caitlin, on the other hand, was never able to get into a groove. First, she had two babies, both of whom were in the NICU and unable to nurse. She had no option but pumping. She spent her days in the hospital pumping and her evenings at home pumping. She knew she was helping her babies by creating breast milk for them and that's what kept her going. She made it through six weeks of pumping and then she was relieved to turn off the pump.

Pumping at work is never easy, but here are a few tips to make it easier:

- Breast-feeding is your right, so don't feel pressured to end it sooner than you're ready. And don't let others' discomfort deter you from doing what you think is right for you and your baby. Now is a great time to learn that to be a successful working mom you should be aware of your boss and coworkers' point of view, but don't let it push you into doing something that is in direct conflict with your beliefs.
- If you don't have an office with a door that shuts, make arrangements with your boss or human resources department to find a quiet private place. Also make sure there is a refrigerator available to you.
- Keep extra milk bags in your desk for the day you forget to bring in your portable bottles.

- Keep an extra shirt at work for the inevitable time that you will leak through your clothes.
- Make sure to keep your breast-feeding times clear on your schedule. Conference calls and meetings that delay your pumping session will get you off schedule and make the entire process even more difficult. Try to use those thirty minutes of pumping time to clear your head or get organized for the rest of the day. It's probably the only private time you'll have. Try to savor it.
- If it seems overwhelming and impossible to pump at work, don't beat yourself up about supplementing with formula. Kim was obsessed with breast-feeding and really enjoyed it. She realized only after her son quit on her (he pushed her away at ten months old) that the reason he ate every three hours until he was six months was because he was starving. He probably would have slept more, and she would have got more work done, if she had just supplemented with formula during the day.

hello . . . i'm not *just* a mom

Jennifer never thought that she would feel insecure after having her baby. Never one to notice if anyone was noticing her, she didn't consider how her role in the world would change once she became a mom. She can honestly say there wasn't even a fleeting thought about how she would feel about being treated differently. So, imagine her surprise when six months after having Adam she realized that the first question clients now asked was about her son. People she had represented for years seemed surprised that she was more interested in discussing what was in the business section than the latest Super Nanny. Her younger staff now treated her differently, a little more distant and respectful, a little less peer-like. Gone was the Monday morning gossip over coffee, she was now a ma'am. And, embarrassingly, she missed the whistles she once ducked on the way to the office—they had dried up tout suite. It was like she aged twenty years in the three months she had been on bed rest. Once she began taking note of how people were interacting with her, she began to feel more like an unrelatable archetype and less like the fun career girl she once was.

Wait just a minute!

She liked that girl and she wanted her back. But the truth was that she was now a mom, who had to run out to relieve the nanny, who had to schedule appointments with the pediatrician, who couldn't ever join the team after work for drinks. The anger at becoming someone else turned into depression. And the erasing of her old self began. She began wearing the kinds of clothes she thought she should wear, the heels were put in the back of the closet, and her hair was now a warmer brown instead of butter blond. Eventually, the paranoia about becoming invisible at work became reality.

Now this story may sound shallow, but even if you could care less about ever wearing that Catherine Malandrino dress you saw in *InStyle*, you must have some version of Jennifer's story. Most of us go through a huge identity change—and crisis—when we become a mother. The way others treat you contributes to an already shaky self-esteem. Let's be honest: People have a lot of baggage when it comes to the concept of mom. At work, this could manifest itself in many ways. Your assistant, ten years younger than you, now sees a maternal figure and starts unloading her personal problems on you. Your boss, anxious about her own mothering skills, judges your priorities unfairly and pressures you to take on too much work. Your human resources director, with his history of female employees that don't return to work post-baby, constantly questions your commitment to the company.

We talk a lot in our books about the key to success being finding and projecting your authentic self. To navigate any big change, personal or professional, take time to reconnect with who you really are—now—not the girl you used to be.

the word

LINDA BRIERTY, THERAPIST

It seems like so many of us have a hard time, especially at the beginning, easing into our new identity as a mom. Do you have any thoughts about that to share with our readers?

The old version of motherhood was one of selfless martyrdom, sacrifice, the loss of self, and the complete devotion of life to the children and family. Obviously, this could create resentment and limit a woman's potential. The new paradigm of motherhood is seen as an expansion of the sense of self, not a negation of the original identity. Nothing has to be lost! There is much to be gained—greater depths of love, compassion, and empathy, and selflessness in the best possible sense of the word—seeing the world beyond the limitations of the individual ego. Motherhood can facilitate opening our hearts to all beings. We can find strengths and potentials we never knew we had in our role as mother. We can also learn to mother ourselves every step of the way, and avoid the common pitfall of self-neglect. We can remember to nurture all of our relationships simultaneously to maintain a support network while raising a child. Keep your interests and passions alive to the extent that you can. In fact, you may find that motherhood makes you more effective; you may even manage your time better than before—because there will be less of it! You may also find that your child inspires you to be your best self, emotionally and professionally, in terms of health and personal development. Parenthood can also be a deeply spiritual and transformational event, if we see it as a gift and practice gratitude. Not only will you be raising your child, your child will be raising you.

FIFTEEN WORKING MOM MANTRAS

1. I can't control everything.
2. I am doing my best.
3. I love my family and I love myself.
4. I can't care what others think.
5. I am relevant and important at work and at home.
6. I don't have to do everything.
7. Nothing is perfect.
8. I deserve time for myself.
9. When I take care of myself, I'm taking care of my family.
10. I am not ruining my child because I go to work.
11. It's OK to love working.
12. I can ask for help.
13. Other people can do things as well as I can.
14. My career is as important as my husband's.
15. My child does not love the nanny more than me.

are you in high gear already?

Now that you're back in action, opportunities for advancement and big projects are going to come your way. And projects that you would have campaigned for before you had a baby, need to be carefully considered now before you accept. Your priorities have changed. You can make different choices and still be a great career girl. What if you're asked to fly to London for three days to pitch a new client? What if you need to work over a weekend to finish a presentation? You have a baby who needs every second of your spare time, so the answer is always "no," right? *Wrong.* The answer is actually "maybe."

Before accepting or declining, find out how high profile the assignment is and how much your boss and, more important, your company is invested in it, ask yourself if you are the best person for the job, and try to figure out how much of an impact a success would have on your career in the short and long term. Most important, talk to your significant other about the opportunity to see if it's even possible for you to commit any additional time. And don't forget to do a gut-check as Mompreneur Felicia Watson advises: "I would say that if there's a project that I'm stressing about because of the deadline and I have some inner turmoil that's carried over to my family time, I would pass on it. My children are only young once and I don't want to miss it or be preoccupied during that precious time with them."

Ten Dos and Don'ts When It Comes to Taking Your Child to Work

1. Don't expect your child to entertain herself.
2. Do bring toys, books, art supplies, and projects to keep her busy.
3. Don't plan on having coworkers or subordinates watch your child.
4. Do let people visit briefly with your child.
5. Don't let your child get hungry.
6. Do come prepared with a selection of snacks to keep him busy and full.
7. Don't plan for several hours in the office with your child.
8. Do arrange for a short window of time.
9. Don't let your child distract coworkers.
10. Do leave as soon as it's disruptive.

is it working at home?

Family stresses are going to arise the day you go back to work because many of you are one of *two* working parents who are trying to share responsibility. In fact, this is such a challenge that we devote an entire chapter to it later in the book. But here's a little preview. When you have children, everything gets dirtier, the laundry triples (or even quadruples), the quick trips to the supermarket become major—sometimes multi-cart—excursions, and new appointments and obligations begin to fill the family calendar. With both parents working, there isn't that much time you are physically home to do what needs to get done. There are now many more things to discuss, coordinate, agree on, plan for, and delegate, but less quiet time together to do that. And who can deal with talking about anything while getting breakfast together at the same time as dressing for an important client meeting? The vision of a family rushing out the door in the morning is a cliché that is exploited by every cereal bar and frozen waffle maker in the country, but it happens in millions of households every day and reflects our harried reality. And when it comes to keeping everything running smoothly at home, do you feel like you're always doing more than your partner? (Single moms, we know you put in 110 percent every day.) You are not crazy. Chances are good that if you have a husband, you are doing more work than he is.

Just look at the stats and you'll see it is not your imagination. A recent study from the University of Wisconsin's National Survey of Families and Households found that in households where the wife and the husband have full-time jobs, the woman does twenty-eight hours of housework and the man only sixteen. And this doesn't count child care, where it has been demonstrated in multiple studies that the mother does triple the work. Why? Because we're women and we're often better at multitasking, organizing, being patient, thinking ahead, putting ourselves last. We absolutely hate to generalize about gender issues, but this is really true: Women are better at running a house while also working than men. It could be just the way we're wired, or it could be that all of us have set the bar too low for men. Why is it OK for them to do less housework when we work the same hours?

Because women are naturally caretakers, we are too often the solution to making an unworkable situation tolerable. We take too much on. We agree to pick up prescriptions during our lunch hour, drop the dog off at the vet before work, cancel our business trip because of a scheduling conflict, and find ourselves doing the third load of laundry even though we did the first two.

The trick to making it all work—without resenting, or worse, hating each other—is a combination of systems and constant communication. You're a professional woman, bring some of that organizational spirit home and post a family calendar. Put everything on there, from doctor's appointments and vacations to business trips and veterinary checkups. Go over the calendar together so you both can prioritize the responsibilities and have a conversation about what is really important to each of you.

Make a list of household chores—and we mean all of them. The big, small, daily, monthly, and yearly: walking the dog, changing the sheets, going to the dump, replacing the diaper genie, making dinner, packing lunch, buying seasonal clothing, vacuuming the house. Everything you can think of should go on there. Then pull out the calendar and start splitting things up. If it's too overwhelming to look at five months from now, then start with this month. When it starts looking like fifty-fifty, then you're getting better. Keep going. Make a list of all the people whom you give household responsibilities to—that could be a plumber, lawn mower, babysitter, day care provider, nanny, or relative that cares for your baby while you're at work, a housecleaner, even the neighborhood teenager who cleans out your garage—and split up who is the point person for each.

We were taught growing up that we can have it all. Sure you can, but maybe not all of it today. What you can aspire to rather than un-attainable perfection is a work/home situation that goes smoothly *most* of the time.

girl talk

SINGLE MOM TRIALS AND TRIUMPHS

Hillary McCarthy did not intend to be a single mother. But when her son's father backed out of the relationship and parenting responsi-bilities within just a few months of the birth, she had to reconfigure not just her life but her definition of family. We wanted to include her in this book because she inspires us. Through a lot of hard work she has embraced her role as sole provider for her son and created a support system that works.

What kind of help do you have (hopefully lots)?
It was critically important for me to have a presence at Luke's pre-school and get to know the other families, so I take him to school three times a week at 8:30 a.m. before work. I have hired a nanny who picks Luke up in the afternoon, does our laundry, and stays un-til I get home at 5:30. She keeps the house neat, but because she is taking care of Luke, she doesn't do any real cleaning.

Did you know right away what kind of help you needed?
It took me a while to figure it all out. Initially, I worked out of my home as a consultant and had lots of time to devote to my son. It meant I caught up at night while he was sleeping, but it was worth it to me both financially and emotionally. I will say, though, those first two years took a toll on me. I lost myself in the mix—com-pletely giving up working out, I didn't sleep enough and became

depressed. I was trying to take care of everything in our home and lives by myself and allowing no time for me to do the things I loved. I am in a much better place now that I make that time to work out and socialize.

Since you are doing much of this alone, do you have a few systems that you could share with moms just trying to figure this out?

Our nightly ritual now begins in the kitchen. Luke "helps" me while I prepare our dinner. It's a great time for us to reconnect and I get to hear about his day. When you work full-time, every second counts. As for school mornings? Those are tough. I allow Luke to watch TV while I shower and get dressed. Then it's breakfast and racing to get him ready.

How do you fit in the household stuff (paying bills, cleaning) without a second set of hands?

Hmmm. I clean the bathroom when Luke is bathing! It keeps him company and allows me to multitask. I make our beds as soon as we get up; my eyes probably aren't even open. I handle the kitchen while I'm prepping meals. So, if something's on the stove, I'm cleaning out the fridge. Multitasking all the time. I pay bills online, either from my office during lunch or in the evenings.

What is the biggest surprise you've had since becoming a working mother?

How much I can accomplish in a single day! I never gave myself credit for this until very recently, but now I'm becoming proud of what I've accomplished for me and Luke.

Anything else you want to share?

I am a different person than who I was before Luke, but I think I veered too far away. It is so incredibly important to maintain who you are, at your core. I've only recently seen glimpses of my old self, and I'm working hard to bring her back. Also, let go of the ideals of family and embrace what it really is. What I have with my son is beautiful and I cherish it.

center yourself for success

When writing this chapter we reviewed long lists of what working moms could do to set themselves up for a successful go at their new role. We had notes about hiring housecleaners and dog walkers, skipping bake sales, and saying no to volunteer work. We realized we were encouraging you to pursue a work/life balance that would be both expensive (defeating the purpose of why many of us work in the first place) and unsatisfying. Back to square one we went and used this chapter to offer you methods of centering yourself as a working mom. After all, you have much, much more on your plate now and the best way to deal with that is to nurture yourself and your spirit and learn to deal with the emotional hurdles of your new dual roles.

the painful compromises: missing moments

The bummer is that children go through huge changes over the first few years and it is inevitable that working moms will miss a milestone or two. While you are working on the annual budget, your child could have just taken his first step or said her first word. Health insurance agent and mom Lorraine Nellis shares this: "The truth is that if you work, someone else will share some of the milestone moments, but know that you will still have your own great memories."

What you have to tell yourself is this: The first time you see your baby take a step is your first time. And there will be developments that you will witness over their lifetime that are just as amazing compared to every other debut you may have missed.

And get rid of the guilt! (Guilt is such a pervasive problem for working moms that we devote a whole section to it in Chapter Eight.)

We spoke to working mother Maria Morris, who struggled with guilt for the first years of working and parenting. Maria said, "I have always said that being raised Catholic removed the blood from my veins and replaced it with guilt. Being a working mother solidified that! So it's hard for me to admit this, but the moment I drop the kids off and get back into the car, I get a chance to breathe. I feel free! I feel like what I was before kids. I change the satellite radio from Disney to Howard Stern (yeah, I listen to him) and drink my coffee. I look down at myself to see how much snot or food remnants I have on me. I fix my hair and head off. Yeah, it's a tough, tough choice, but the fact is I also can't wait to pick them up at the end of the day."

That isn't to say it isn't painful or doesn't make you regret—hopefully briefly—the decision to go back to work. It hurts to miss the signs of your baby growing up, but that is at the heart of the compromise to be a working mom. You have to make peace with the fact that there will be things you miss, but your relationship with your child transcends any one step. Maria recommends cutting back on how much time and energy you put into chores because she found that "by simplifying the world around me I don't miss as many of those little moments, and there are so many of them."

THOUGHTS FROM ALLISON TAYLOR, A WORKING MOM

When I was eighteen and pregnant, I began college. Thanks to the support of my mother, who watched my son while I attended classes, I completed my bachelor's degree by the time he was two.

I went to work as soon as I graduated, which was a difficult and exhilarating transition. Work demands your attention, but so does your baby and home. I had to learn to become mindful in the role I was playing at any given time and give my all in every area. The thing to accept is that your life is always evolving and changing. You are growing as you cycle through whatever career or family expansion you take on. Before you try to schedule your life, you must prioritize.

The only way to organize and manage is to first decide your center. For every woman this is different. What is important to you? What do you need to see, do, achieve, teach, or discover to feel you are fulfilling your purpose? When your life reflects your highest priorities, your children learn to manage their goals and their talents, and they become competent and dignified individuals. That is what I learned from my mother, who made my education a priority for both of us before she passed away.

I have been through many changes in my home life and my career, but there's always more to learn. There lives a spirit in each of us, the spirit of a unique woman. The only way to honor yourself is to listen to your passions and to love the life you are creating. It is hard to get up so early, to pack the lunches, to concentrate on the presentation, to keep it all together. Only you can define your goals based on your personal mission. Take time to be your own company and remember what you bring to each and every relationship.

It's hard to be a working mom. It's hard to separate from your child when you go to work and it's hard to turn off the office when you come home to the baby. When I was younger, I completely underestimated the importance of doing things for myself that were healthy for my mind, spirit, and body. If you neglect yourself, you'll be trying to run your family on empty. Be gentle as you grapple with the tough stuff. If it all seems too much, accept a helping hand. As women, we sometimes think if we are not working like dogs to shine in our career while raising stellar children while doing laundry and cooking a gourmet dinner while making dentist appointments as we have the oil changed and balance our checkbooks while spinning plates on our heads . . . we aren't doing anything special. You do not have to prove your stamina to anyone. If we could wear one less hat, let it be the one that is self-critical.

I have found recently in my life, meeting women in all types of careers with all different families, sometimes the best thing we can do for ourselves is to recognize and compliment another woman. See her strength and empathize with her struggles. There is nothing more heartbreaking or detrimental to our success than cutting each other down. Surround yourself with positive and humorous women who are also working moms. We need to celebrate each other.

you can't afford to run yourself ragged

Even if your partner is an excellent co-parent, as the mother of the household, you are its center. You are the touchstone, the constant, the heart of the home. We know how corny that sounds, and believe us, we are cynical urban girls and we don't throw around words like "touchstone" lightly. But we have found even when we don't want to be the one that knows where everything is, when the parent-teacher meeting is scheduled, or who we hire for babysitting on Thursday nights, we are. In addition to being the head of household, emotionally and/or otherwise, you have your career to take care of. As a working mother, you are being judged by your coworkers, many of whom expected you to bag it all for life at home. Some of them may have been counting on it.

As unfair as it may seem, especially when you are running on empty, you have to work harder, better, and smarter in the early days of returning to the office. You need to demonstrate that you haven't lost your ambition, edge, and guts.

How are you going to do all of that—kick butt at work, run your household, be there for your child—if you are run down? The answer quite simply is you can't. It is essential that you take care of yourself both physically and mentally right now. You absolutely must take time for yourself to recharge. Don't think of going to get a massage or taking a few hours on the weekend to see a movie as shirking your responsibilities. Think of those moments alone, and time away from your duties, as doctor's orders. With everything you are doing, you can't afford to get sick or burned out. When you are depleted, you start losing focus, you have a harder time making decisions and getting things done. And let's not forget how quickly you lose your patience and temper when you're tired. On the flipside, when you are well rested after spending a few hours or, even a day, alone you can be fully present at work and home.

And it's really all about being fully present and engaged, isn't it? Be home when you are home and at work when you are at work. The only way to have that focus is by making sure you are not running on empty. So here are your orders from us: Take a break. You, the family and the employer deserve to have your best.

asking for what you need

When we interviewed women for our second book, *The Girl's Guide to Being a Boss Without Being a Bitch*, about their management challenges, most of them included their reluctance to delegate. Some of the women felt they could do tasks quicker, if not better than, their employees. Or they felt uncomfortable telling people what to do. Many felt like the only way to guarantee it was done right was to do it themselves.

We think this unwillingness to take anything off our plates effects us at home just as much as the office. And as with work, if we don't ask for help or delegate tasks, at home we find our list longer at the end of each day. Even if you do a better job cleaning the house, and you don't put the reds in with the whites when you do the laundry, and you cook things that the kids actually eat . . . let your partner take on some of the work. And don't wait for them to ask either, because it might not happen. Just start handing off some tasks, then leave them to it without chiming in with your suggestions, advice, or criticism.

Working mom-raised Amanda Dantico shares this: "My sister and I, and even my father, were all assigned chores when we were old enough. All of us cleaned the bathrooms, did the dishes, laundry, yard work, vacuuming and dusting. My mother didn't want us growing up on fast food, which I thank her for now, but we all had to help cook dinner. My mom keeps a very clean house, but she learned fast that she had to just let it go and know that not all the chores were going to get done."

The key to your success both at work and at home is asking and delegating, because everyone might not be noticing what you are doing. And they, for sure, are not reading your mind. So if you need time or a change in the schedule to accommodate your professional responsibilities, then ask for it. If you need a housecleaner to come in once a month or once a week to help, and you can afford it, then ask for it. If you need your partner to take on more responsibility, then ask for it. Of course, this is the hardest ask of all, so be sure to read about delegating to your partner in Chapter Seven.

WORKING MOMS BLOG

Where these women get the time we will never know, but they are out there. And there are a lot of them. Working women everywhere are blogging about their experiences, challenges, tips, solutions to everyday problems, healthy foods, favorite celebrities, TV shows, and, of course, partners. Most of them have ways for you to contribute your own stories or tips to share, as well as find a community of women going through some of the same things you are experiencing every day. Some of the better blogs and forums can be found on bigger sites that include much more than one woman's personal musings. If you are looking to connect, know you're not alone, or share your own stories, struggles, or triumphs, maybe you can find what you're looking for online in those few free moments for yourself.

Here are five of our favorite mom blogs and sites:

www.workitmom.com—This is what Work It Mom says about itself: "We want Work It, Mom! to speak through your honest, revealing, and inspiring voices and to be the place where other busy professional moms come for advice, support, ideas, and a bit of laughter and relief from the daily juggle of work and family." Once on the Web site, you'll find stories and discussions on topics including careers, money, politics, maternity leave and clothes. And you can read any of the featured blogs or member blogs. You can even start your own.

www.momlogic.com—Much more than just a blog, Momlogic describes itself as "the ultimate destination for Moms who want to know a little bit about a lot of things, but have very little time." You will find blogs and posts in the community section. Other sections include health, entertainment, politics, and beauty. And our favorite part, the daily roundup of some of momlogic's favorite mom blogs—Top Five: Best of the Blogs. There's no time to hit every site every day, momlogic does it for you and gives you the best of the day.

www.workingmomsagainstguilt.com—OK, we liked it just from the name of it. The four women who run the site describe it this way: "We're moms. We work all day, bring home the bacon, and fry it up in a pan. Oh, and while we're at it, we're raising young children, along with our spouses/partners. As any working mom knows, we often battle the big 'G.' Guilt creeps up on us when we least expect it. Join us in our ongoing struggle to resist the guilt and embrace the journey." Once again, you'll not only find their blogs (which are not only about being a working mother but can touch on politics or products or whatever they might be thinking about that day) but links to other sites you might find helpful, entertaining, or interesting.

www.workingmomsblog.com—Don't be confused. When you go on here, it'll say "Work It Mom" at the top, but these are two different sites. And this is the site that describes itself: "Many different voices writing about one thing in all of its complexity—motherhood. We are women, moms, wives, workers, managers, etc. and we want to share our stories." With more than fifteen working moms blogging, you're almost sure to find a voice that speaks to you. And the site also gives a list of links to "Working Moms Around the Web," a great resource for research and information—and more blogs, too.

www.divinecaroline.com—This is a site for women by women. It has stories and forums on all topics, including parenthood and working mothers. In those sections you'll find discussions on controversial parenting styles, child care, and prioritizing, among other things. And here you can stop being a mom and a working mom for a moment if you want. As the site says about itself, "Our dream is to give you a place to come together and express yourselves. What brings you joy. What breaks your heart. Makes you giggle. What pisses you off. Confuses you. Entertains you. What keeps you strong. And if all that sounds too heady, remember we're also discussing stuff like sketchy relatives and good kissers."

And of course you can always visit our favorite blog, www.girls guidetobusiness.com.

the right to change your mind

We have the power to make choices that will affect how we work, how we parent, and how we want to live. We do it all the time. Too often we forget we're allowed to change our minds. If there's one thing we've learned from writing this book, it's that you really don't know anything until you know. You think you will want to stay home after you've had your baby only to realize you can't wait to get back to work. You think you will love breast-feeding, only to discover that you keep getting clogged milk ducts and you hate it. These scenarios point to the larger issues. We're all just trying to figure it out, and even with the most thorough planning and advance research, the solutions you've come up with often just don't work.

Don't feel bad about it. Just try something else. Do more research, ask friends and colleagues for their ideas. You have the power to change your situation, just know that the changes could take years to happen. It took Eileen seven years to get her family an international posting (see The Word, Chapter Seven) and Nicole is still trying to find the work situation that will make her happiest at home (see Girl Talk, Chapter Nine). None of this is easy, but here are some things to keep in mind:

- If you know something is not working, don't wait for it to fix itself. It won't. Kim's son was having problems in school, and instead of dealing with it right away, as she would any problem at work, she trusted the teachers knew more than she did. They didn't. Once she intervened and put new systems in place, her son began to flourish.

- Be willing to adapt the system you've created. As your kids grow up, and as your responsibilities change at work, you will need a new schedule and a new way to distribute the responsibilities.

- You have the power to make radical change. If you hate your job because it doesn't allow you to be flexible, start looking for a new job. Be willing to take less money if it offers more flexibility. Time is worth money to working mothers.

just say "no"

Many of us say yes to whatever is asked of us. Whether we are conditioned to be people pleasers or it's just in our nature, the consequences are the same—we do too much. Before agreeing to anything, look at what's already on your plate. Then look at the timing of the favor, assignment, task, chore that is being asked of you.

Because you have so little time now, you have to become highly selective about what you take on and sometimes you are going to have to say no, which is very difficult for most of us. We interviewed Jane Miller, a single mother of two children and the editor at a major publishing house. When we asked her how she manages to get everything done at work she shared this: "Sometimes I just have to stay a little later to work on a major project, but the key for me is that I am extremely efficient at the office. I don't do unnecessary lunch dates and try to make smart benefit/cost choices, where the cost side of the equation is my time and the benefit side is the revenue I'll bring in. Knowing that I have to leave at 5:30 has made me focus hard on what I choose to take on. It has also taught me how to say no to various things, not always easy. In fact, the other day someone got annoyed with me when he asked a favor that I couldn't do. Okay, he was annoyed, but then he has a stay-at-home wife to look after his house and kids."

> **TEN SIGNS THAT THINGS NEED READJUSTING IN YOUR LIFE**
>
> 1. You never have a second to yourself.
> 2. You are angry much of the time.
> 3. You constantly fight with your partner over the chores.
> 4. You micromanage your employees and your spouse.
> 5. You resent your kids for needing attention from you.
> 6. You agree to unnecessary business trips just to get away.
> 7. Around Sunday evening, you begin to dread going to work.
> 8. On Friday afternoon, you begin to dread the weekend with the family.
> 9. You are exhausted most of the time.
> 10. Social time with friends is a distant memory.

ten things to do for yourself

We do not make or take enough time for ourselves. In fact, a study conducted by the Families and Work Institute on the changing workforce found that modern dads spend 1.3 hours each workday on themselves while moms only take .9 hours. Depressingly, this number is obviously shrinking because back in 1977 a similar study found that moms had 1.6 hours for themselves. The thing is, we need downtime to recharge so we can not only enjoy life more but we will have more to give. Here are ten things you can try doing for yourself, ideally by yourself.

- Read an escapist novel. You want something entertaining that will take your mind off of everything you have on your to-do list. Caitlin's secret is young adult novels, because there isn't anything more relaxing than reading about heroines stressing about proms, boys, or getting into college. Ahh . . . those were the days.
- Watch all of the television shows you can't seem to find time for on DVD. Make sure *Friday Night Lights*, *Mad Men*, and the first season of *Veronica Mars* are on your list. Such good television.
- Lunch with old friends. We are talking about getting together with people who knew you before, during, and after your new life as a working mother. It is fun to talk and laugh about the days that you now realize were, in retrospect, really easy.
- Stretch, take up yoga, or get to the gym. Getting physically active can take your mind off things while boosting your confidence and energy and reducing stress. Nothing bad about that.
- Schedule a weekly breakfast with your significant other. Okay, we know this is all about you time, but it's nice to reconnect and nothing kills a relationship faster than spending time talking only about errands, chores, and bills. Boooorrring.
- Negotiate to sleep late on a weekend day. Hey, you're exhausted and knowing you won't have to get up at the crack of dawn on Saturday or Sunday can get you through a tough week.
- Start walking at lunch. Sounds silly, but with your iPod filled with your personalized playlist, it can be beyond relaxing and rejuvenating to get some fresh air.
- Get up a little earlier and spend an hour alone. Read a book, the paper, or just tune out over that first cup of delicious coffee. A quiet house is a nice way to enter the day.
- While most of us don't have the time or money for a spa day, an hour with a masseuse feels pretty great.

- Start planning a weekend away, either with your spouse, alone, or with your best friend. Just having a personal trip on the calendar—even if it is six months away—can be a reminder that downtime is coming up.

knowing how you work best

Time to be honest. How many of us, pre- or post-pregnancy, work eight, ten, or twelve hours straight? Many of us put in a solid three, and then take a lunch break, getting back to work half speed for a few hours, then full speed again after a coffee break. Others work through lunch, crashing around four and being pretty useless until the end of the day. At our office, we've noticed that the staff is a little slow to start but really focused from eleven until seven. In fact, we have one employee who only works well if she comes in around ten in the morning, so we've switched her hours to accommodate her.

Whatever your rhythm is, after you have a baby it will change, so start paying attention to the times of day that you are most productive and see if you can work your job around it. It's not always easy if you find yourself wide awake and focused at 3 a.m., but hopefully your good hours will intersect with your on-the-clock hours. If you have the kind of job and company that offers flexibility, then you may want to consider shifting your schedule around to maximize your most productive self. If not, then at least tackle the tough assignments when you are at your best. We had a boss who encouraged us to work through our to-do lists in the morning, crossing off the most challenging tasks first. Leave the brainless work on your list to do when you are, in fact, brainless.

girl talk

We met Jen Groover (www.jengroover.com) at the Pennsylvania's Governor's Conference for Women and were impressed not only by her success (she's invented like a zillion products!) but by her attitude. She may well be the most positive person we've ever met. It turns out she wasn't always this way. She started out as a fitness expert. Right out of college she opened a gym and was training clients, teaching aerobics, and competing nationally in aerobics competitions. After two national competitions in 2000, Jen returned home physically and mentally exhausted—which was typical for her after a big event. She figured she'd recover in a couple of weeks like she'd done every time before, but it didn't happen. As a matter of fact, she proceeded to get worse and worse. She dragged herself (literally) from doctor to doctor who kept telling her she was fine. She knew she wasn't fine and began doing her own research. She finally found a doctor who was willing to consider that this twenty-seven-year-old woman in peak physical condition was suffering from chronic fatigue syndrome. Her tests were conclusive and her doctor was declarative. If she didn't change her life immediately, she wouldn't ever heal.

For the first time in her life, Jen was terrified. She was used to relying on herself, as she'd been on her own since her late teens. She had opened and run a successful business and was constantly giving her female clients advice about how to start businesses for themselves. She knew she was an ideas person but had no idea how to turn her ideas into money, even though she watched her clients do exactly that. She sold her gym to her partner and began studying intellectual property. At the same time, she went on a journey of self-exploration to help repair her damaged body.

She credits yoga, massage therapy, and reiki with the repair to her body, and her new positive attitude came from working diligently to change her thought processes. She makes a conscious decision every day to be a positive thinker. Now she's the mother of four-and-a-half-year-old twins, and we spoke to Jen about her hard-fought battle to get healthy and centered in her life.

We heard your story. However, it doesn't sound as if you're going any slower than you did before you got sick. What has changed?
I still do as much as I did before, maybe more with the kids involved, but I do everything differently. I've learned to say no after too many years of saying yes because I didn't want to disappoint people. Or because I thought they wouldn't like me if I said no. What I learned is that if I didn't prioritize my health and take care of myself, I would be of no use to anyone—not my employees, my husband, or my children.

How do you take care of yourself?
For starters, I eat healthy, am active—no more gym, lots of running after kids—take vitamins, and drink acai berry juice for the antioxidants. I have also learned how to change my thought process away from negative thinking (how am I ever going to get this all done?) to positive thinking (I can get this all done if I do x, y, and z). Although for me it's more important sometimes to *not* do x, y, or z. I've learned that my body has limits, and if I need to take a day off after a big adrenaline-charged event, then I not only will, but I better because otherwise it will negatively impact whatever comes after it. I am much smarter about setting boundaries now.

But how did you get to this new place?
It was a total spiritual journey for me and it was extremely difficult. I poured myself into it 1,000 percent and tried to rid myself of layers of negative thinking and baggage from my childhood. It wasn't easy, but it worked. I made a conscious decision to vibrate on the highest, most positive level every single day.

How has motherhood changed you?
I have a completely different vision of perfection than I used to have. When I was younger, I strove to be perfect in every single thing. Now I am striving to be successful and honor the commitments that I make to my family and business relationships to the best of my ability.

it's never quiet
on the home front

Now that you're centered, you need some real, practical tips because, frankly, life is a little insane now. And it isn't going to slow down anytime soon. Sure, the diapers will go away, but they will be replaced by accidents (kinda gross but true). Kindergarten begins but so does pinkeye. Unless you develop at least something resembling a "go with the flow" attitude, you will absolutely lose your mind. In this chapter we talk about the typical schedule of a working family, including the new significance of breakfast and dinner. We share tips from busy moms on how to make life a little easier, and we'll touch on how your responsibilities at home could impact your job. As two working moms with two companies between us, we know how the lines blur between work and home these days, but there are strategies that will help all parties—your family, your boss, your employees, and yourself—can have their needs met. At least most of the time.

is a smooth morning possible?

All of those images you see in commercials and movies—the harried working moms, half-dressed for work, running around feeding the family, and jumping out of the way of flying oatmeal—are inspired by truth. Most of us only have two hours in the morning, if that, to get ourselves showered and dressed, the children up dressed and fed, day care bags or lunches packed, and household chores taken care of. It's a lot to cram into a little window, and even if we wake up with the best of intentions, stress can lead to arguments and tension. Suddenly, everyone is heading off into the world without the support they need.

Is it possible to do things differently? Of course. But let's start with your attitude about the morning. First things first: Don't hold onto the hope that you will have any time, space, or peace to focus on your own needs once everyone is awake. Your children are going to need and want your full attention and don't care if you are anxious about an upcoming review. Instead of waking up at the first cry or tug at your bedcovers, set the alarm earlier. A half hour, an hour, whatever you need to take care of your needs whether that is showering, ironing, running, meditating, or gathering your thoughts for the upcoming workday. Any little bit of time that you carve out for yourself makes a huge difference in everyone's day. If you are collected while the chaos whirls around you, then you won't easily be thrown off your game in the likely event something goes wrong.

Here are a few additional tips—gathered from talking to working women like you—that may help you ease into the day:

- After you are showered, don't put on your work clothes. Change into sweats to buzz through breakfast and the morning list. Not having to worry about spilled orange juice on your suit or creases in the shirt you just ironed can reduce unnecessary stress.

- Pack lunch or snacks the night before and have everything ready to pop into a backpack. When you do the shopping, pick up things like juice boxes and small bottles of water in bulk ahead of time so they will always be on hand to send off with your kids.
- Get an automatic coffee maker so you can have that first cup seconds after opening your eyes. Okay, this one was from Caitlin, who is admittedly a caffeine addict.
- Feed your kids while they are still in their pajamas so you don't care if (when) they spill their breakfast.
- Take five minutes each morning to review the running household list before you leave for work. It is helpful to know what errands you each have to take care of at lunch or on the way home.
- Eat something healthy with your kids. Too many of us grab something to eat while driving. It isn't good for you, and you're missing quality time with your family.
- Don't expect anything to go smoothly and then be grateful when something does.
- Spend a few minutes every morning focused exclusively on your kids. No multitasking, putting away dishes while you are hurrying them along. If you give them your attention before they head off into the world, it will do wonders for their confidence and self-esteem.

Now the kids are with their caretakers, and it's back to just you. Take a huge breath and clear your head. If there has been some tension between you and your partner, let it go, because in just a little while your office is going to need your full attention. To make the transition, many of the mothers we spoke to stop at their favorite morning spot to pick up a fresh cup of coffee; a few meet a colleague to catch up before going into the office or walk rather than take a cab from the train station. Whatever it is, try to find something, a prework ritual, that signals the end of your mom self and the beginning of your work self.

TEN THINGS YOU SHOULD DO AT HOME TO MAKE YOUR LIFE EASIER

1. Don't do laundry every day.
2. Try giving the kids a bath every other day.
3. Plan meals in advance.
4. Use leftovers for snacks or lunches.
5. Multitask the chores (clean the bathrooms when your kids are in the bath, scrub the kitchen while the pasta water is boiling).
6. Have weekly meetings with your spouse to evenly delegate the chores, appointments, errands, and other household responsibilities.
7. Pay your bills online.
8. Get help whenever you can.
9. Prep for morning at night and for night in the morning.
10. Don't overschedule yourself with obligations (know your limitations).

---

preparing your family for business travel

Business trips are a necessity for many of us, and although our families would rather we stay home, it often isn't possible to opt out. When your children are still infants your first business trip can be a heart-wrenching experience or a welcomed break, depending on the support you have on the home front.

Preparing everyone for an upcoming trip starts with coordinating the schedule with all of the caregivers, most important your partner. If your child is old enough to understand, start telling them a few days before you leave that you are taking a trip but will be back. Gerri Cristantiello tells her husband first, and then as it gets closer to the date she begins to tell her young son. Gerri writes: "I tell him how many nights I will be away and that daddy will take care of him, that I will come back and, most important, that he can call me any time he wants to. So if he misses me or wants to talk to me, he can call me on my cell phone. I tell him how many times he will go to sleep before he sees me."

Expect your partner to push back a little or a lot when you have a business trip on the calendar. As annoying as that may be, most spouses would just rather not do the home stuff solo. Some of our readers suggested that their husbands were anxious about the child care responsibility. Others just felt like their spouses gave them grief because they just didn't want to work as hard as we do. But some maybe just feel ill-equipped to juggle it all without you. Even if you have a completely supportive and confident partner, you might be feeling emotional—sad, anxious, nervous, excited—about leaving. The first trip is always the hardest, but once you return and see that your family is healthy and happy, the house still standing, everyone still loves you, and your spouse hasn't lost his or her mind, you'll be better prepared for the next one.

Business trips are complicated aspects of our job responsibilities because they demand huge sacrifices of your personal time. And, as we know, that personal time isn't just yours to give up anymore. If your job requires you to spend a lot of time on the road and your partner just can't make up for it due to their own careers, then it might be a sign that things need to change. Most jobs, however, don't have you living out of a suitcase, so don't beat yourself up when you do need to take a trip on behalf of the company. And remind a resentful spouse that your job and your salary are important too.

how and why to make the most of a business trip

We have confessed in a few *Girl's Guide* books—including this one—how much we love a business trip. It helps that we actually like what we do most of the time, so that the business part of the trip isn't painful and can even be unexpected fun. We also have identified two pieces of planning that make just about every trip comfortable and relaxing. We make reservations at the best-reviewed restaurants specializing in local fare and we stay at boutique hotels. These are two, sometimes inexpensive, ways that we've discovered make being away from home more pleasant.

Whatever makes a trip more fun for you, add it into the mix as you are planning. Can you sneak in that movie you've been dying to see? Pick up the novel at the airport bookstore that has been getting rave reviews? Are there friends that live locally you could see? If you have any control over your schedule, try to book meetings in such a way that you end up with either a morning or an afternoon to enjoy guilt-free you time.

If you just dread business trips and can't get your head around enjoying them, then know this: Business trips offer both professional and personal opportunities. They are good for business because if you do a good job—contribute at an important meeting, learn something crucial that you can share with the team back at the office, meet a potential client, land new business—you are making a statement to your boss that you are an asset. Trips away from the office can also help your career in the bigger picture. When you travel, you are expanding your network of contacts and that can help you far beyond your current position at your current company. Make the most of being out there by setting up meetings, drinks, meals with people in your field. Do research ahead of time. Are there people you want to know in that city? Are there people in your network who could make an introduction before you get to town? Having contacts around the country in your industry can be a huge resource for you down the road when you need advice, job opportunities, connections, guidance, or recommendations. Make the most of each trip by thinking bigger about your career. So get enough sleep, stay in places you love, carve out a little time for yourself to recharge, and appreciate the time you have been given to expand your career.

Business trips also offer opportunities for personal growth as well because at no other time will you have a chunk of time alone. You don't know how great that is until you find yourself sitting on the edge of your bed in a quiet hotel room deciding between watching a movie or taking a hot shower. We mothers are so conditioned to the constant interruptions, that to have the mental and emotional space to reflect on anything is a gift. So when you are on a business trip, take some time to think about your career and ask yourself some questions. What's working and what isn't? How can you contribute more or pull back a little? Are you still inspired by what you do or is it time for a change? Draft an action plan for how to take charge of the direction of your career a little. Our third book, *The Girl's Guide to Kicking Your Career into Gear*, was inspired by women who were looking for ways to take charge of their professional lives. If you find yourself with some space to start thinking about it . . . take advantage of it.

family vacations are sometimes not a vacation

When Caitlin and Andrew took their kids on their first vacation, she came back needing one. It wasn't that she didn't enjoy the twins or being away; it was that she made the mistake of trying to do it all. She tried to juggle "relaxing" with her family while keeping track at things at work and finishing up a book proposal. Don't make the mistake of going into a family trip thinking it's going to be filled with hours of free time. Afternoons when everyone else kicks back and lets you work on the laptop is a pipe dream. Debbie Shandel concurs: "Unfortunately there is no such thing as a true vacation. The BlackBerry beckons at every turn. I try to answer the quick questions on the go but reserve the longer and more research-laden responses for at night after the kids are asleep. I must admit I am not that great with boundaries between work and vacation and that is something that I need to work on. You know it's bad when your five-year-old says, 'Put down the BlackBerry, mommy, and come on the water slide!!!' "

We should all make more of an effort to log off. Kids want and deserve our full attention because they likely only get it in bits and pieces most of the time. If you don't give them what they need, they will jump up and down, start an argument, or send some other signal that what they need is *you*. It's no one's fault, it's just the way it is for working families. So when you are with them 24/7, they are excited and most likely won't be leaving you alone to work.

Plan to check out from work—at least the majority of the time—when you are on vacation by preparing everyone from your assistant to your clients. Wrap up loose ends, finish projects, and schedule meetings with your reports to go over to-do lists, provide your boss with an overview of where things stand, and what is going to be done while you are away. If possible, try to check in with the team once a day and tell everyone that you'll occasionally be checking e-mail. Even if a day goes by where you are incommunicado, knowing that you are making an effort will ease even the most anxious team member. So you don't come back completely stressed out, set reasonable expectations for yourself as well. Know that your job when on a trip with your family is to be the mom, and it will be very difficult to do more than that.

truth: kids get sick

They all get sick, especially if your kids are at day care. In the winter, there might be months when someone is out once or twice a week with something. There is the ridiculously contagious pinkeye that seems to go 'round and 'round the classroom and the lingering cough that makes a brutal return just as you're leaving for the office. There are the weird diseases (fifth's—have you heard of it?) and the seemingly endless winter sniffles. Sometimes it may seem that, literally, there is always something.

Cold and flu season is especially difficult for us. In 2007 *Working Mother* magazine conducted a survey on this very issue. It was discovered that nearly 50 percent of the respondents agreed that the work/life balance is jeopardized during this time because although 33 percent of us have sent our children to school sick, 70 percent of us are wracked with guilt about doing it. With the most common reason being moms can't afford to take the day off thanks to unpaid sick days, most families face an impossible decision.

And, yes, it is no surprise this affects working moms more than dads. In fact, in a 2003 study, the Kaiser Family Foundation found that 49 percent of moms miss work when taking care of a sick child compared to only 30 percent of dads.

We asked several of the women we interviewed about this issue and most of them agreed that in their households they were the ones who either stayed home with a sick child or were responsible for arranging the coverage. When pressed for details, a few of them owned up to the fact that they felt strongly that children needed their mothers when they were sick. Others said that they were the ones who knew how best to navigate the pediatrician, insurance company, and pharmacy. And most of the women took on the responsibility of a sick child without a single discussion with their spouse about that being fair.

For those of you who take this on without thought, know this: The choice to always be the one staying home could be impacting your career. If it's your choice then that's great, but if you are the one missing an important meeting or the third day of work because you don't feel comfortable having anyone else take care of your child or, worse, you buy that your spouse's career is more important, then wait a minute. Days home with a sick child are something to be negotiated. When it looks like things are heading in that direction, pull out the Outlook and see who has the more flexible morning, day, or week ahead of them? Can you split the day, with one of you taking the morning shift at home while the other does the afternoon? If both of you are maxed out, do you have another set of hands to call in?

The point is, the challenge of having a sick child who needs to be home during the workweek is one to be shared. It really isn't up to you to solve the problem, and it is wrong that this too often falls into the mother's lap. So you don't leave the discussion to the last minute when you have a sniffling child and a spouse halfway out the door, have a contingency plan in place for emergencies. Do you have a trustworthy neighbor, best friend, relative, or babysitter with a flexible schedule who can jump in at the last minute? If not, let the negotiations begin.

caitlin shares her absolutely worst week ever

I am sharing this story because I want you to know the truth that even if you use all of the useful strategies we offer, things can still go awry. You have no control over most things that happen in life, especially when you have children. To set the scene of this Worst Week Ever, my twins were almost four. For those of you who haven't been around four-year-olds, they are walking, talking, and intentionally not-listening little bundles of nonstop energy. It started on a Saturday morning when my daughter, Taylor, woke up with the early signs of conjunctivitis in her left eye (a very contagious condition that can require antibiotic drops). Knowing that unless she was on the drops for twenty-four hours she couldn't go to school on Monday, we rushed her to the hospital for a prescription. After a two-hour wait, the emergency room doctor confirmed the diagnosis and gave me the drops, telling me to put them only in the affected eye. I begged her for an extra prescription for my son Declan just in case (since, as I said, this is a very contagious condition), but she refused (guess she didn't want to lose her medical license).

We started the antibiotics that afternoon and, because the infection was very mild, it looked clear by Sunday afternoon. This was a huge relief because I was scheduled for jury duty on Monday, Tuesday, and Wednesday and Andrew was on a book deadline, which meant the kids absolutely had to go to school.

On Monday morning, Taylor cried from the bedroom "My eye!" and we rushed in to see that sure enough her right eye was now infected. To make this all just a little better, moments later Declan shouted "My eye!" He had contracted pink-eye too. So I help get the kids dressed while Andrew was close to crying at the kitchen table, knowing that his writing day has gone out the window, only to be replaced by taking care of two four-year-olds too contagious to leave the house. He took them to the doctor's office to get Declan's prescription and I left for jury duty. While trying to get out of sitting for a four-week trial, I got an e-mail from Andrew telling me that when coming back from the doctor's office, the kids were fighting to open a door and Taylor's toe got jammed underneath it, pulling part of the nail off.

I was released a little early that day and rushed home to look at the eye, toe, and other eye and to see if Andrew was still alive. He had done an excellent job cleaning and wrapping Taylor's toe, so we thought it would be okay until about 7 p.m., when it looked much worse and we decided a trip to the emergency room was in order. So Andrew took her to the emergency room and was there until 2 a.m. And no one wants to be in an emergency room in New York City (or, really, anywhere) at 2 a.m.

Monday: Zero work got done.

By Tuesday morning, Declan's eye was cleared and I brought him to school before going down to serve my second day of jury duty. While Andrew was taking care of Taylor and Declan was playing at school, I was actually selected for a trial, even though I thought for sure that I would be released once I told all of the lawyers that I had found someone guilty the last time I served. I guess that made me even more appealing because I was among the first selected. We all got let go for lunch, and when I told Andrew that I was on a jury he just about broke down on the phone after having spent five hours trying to convince Taylor that staying inside was loads more fun than going to the park with the other kids. After a roller coaster of an afternoon, the jurors were miraculously dismissed, thanks to a little game of chicken between the lawyers that ended in a settlement. I was beyond relieved.

Tuesday: Zero work got done, panic set in, and Andrew and I started fighting.

So, now it was Wednesday morning. Andrew brought Declan to school and I brought Taylor to the doctor's for a follow-up visit on the toe. The nurse looked at it and said it was in great shape, but when the doctor took a peek she saw an infection under the nail and recommended that we go to a plastic surgeon as soon as possible. What?! A plastic surgeon? So I brought Taylor home while we waited for the appointment and Andrew started getting ready to take her. Thankfully, he does the tough doctor's visits with the kids because frankly I just can't handle it. So he brought Taylor to the plastic surgeon, who took off most of the nail on her big toe, and I picked up Declan from school.

Wednesday: Zero work got done, full-blown anxiety attacks and lots of arguing.

Taylor was still home on Thursday, Declan was off to school. I brought her into the office so that I could finish up a few proposals and answer some of the hundreds of e-mails that I couldn't deal with reading on my BlackBerry.

Thursday: Some work got done. Thank God.

On Friday, I took Taylor for a follow-up visit at the plastic surgeon and, thankfully, we were in the clear. She was on the way to being healed and could now take a bath and return to school on Monday. One would think that, maybe, for a few hours during her nap I could get work done, but no, the preschool scheduled a training for the teachers that afternoon—wouldn't you know it—so we had to pick Declan up. Both kids were back at home.

Friday: A tiny little bit of work got done.

And I was counting down the hours until Monday morning at 8:01, when I turn the kids over to the very capable teachers at The Children's Garden.

Lessons Learned: Don't panic when things start going south because there is really nothing you can do about it most of the time. Do what you can to make things better for the people in your life and at work. Don't beat yourself up over things out of your control and, most important, the key to dealing with any crises personal or professional is good communication. Be clear about what you need and what you can do and stick to what you promise.

working with your child's school

You've worked so hard to balance the schedules between your office and your home. Now there's the oft-forgotten factor—school. How much of your time is the school expecting? What is a must and what can be missed?

Let's start with the basics. They expect you to help your children with homework, be engaged with the lessons, appreciate the job of the teachers, drop off and pick up on time, and respect the rules of the school. They will want you to come to parent-teacher meetings. Beyond that, they could expect you to help fund-raise, attend Parent Teacher Association meetings, make costumes for the spring play, or help build the new jungle gym over the weekend. Every school has spoken and unspoken expectations for parental participation. The trick is to figure them out, do what you can, and not take on any more than you can handle.

Ask the director or principal of the school what events they are planning over the course of the year that they would expect parents to attend or help with. See how far in advance you can schedule a parent-teacher meeting, so you can secure a lunchtime slot. Ask what activities they would ideally like parents to participate in or contribute to (this would be the originally unsaid expectations). Ask if there are family barbecues, bake sales, or fund-raising events in the works. Preschool director Susan Stein advises parents to "Try to participate in at least one classroom activity over the year. Kids are so proud when it's their parents who are reading a story, going on a trip with the class, or doing a cooking project with their friends. If the school has fund-raisers or regularly scheduled meetings, try to participate in some way and if you can't attend, at the very least acknowledge your regret that you won't be attending."

You want to know everything that might require more time from you because only then can you be firm about what you can take on and what you can't. If you are cornered by the teacher one day after school and asked if you are coming in over the weekend to help paint the classroom, chances are that you will say yes without taking the time to figure out if you have the child care at home that would even make it possible. Susan says her teachers "know how busy parents are, so responding to the basics of classroom administration are much appreciated: parents should read all notices that are sent home the first time and respond to any requests promptly, whether it's returning permission slips, sign-up sheets, labeling/checking/updating extra clothing, etc."

The teachers are, in many ways your partner, and their influence is significant, so don't take them for granted. Susan says, "Just acknowledging the work around the classroom, or relating an anecdote from the weekend about some school-related matter tells the teachers you appreciate their efforts. And of course, a spontaneous gift of flowers for the classroom or cookies is always nice too."

is a smooth evening possible?

Some people refer to evening with small children as the witching hour. Either the kids are so excited to see their parents that the adrenaline is making them nuts or their hunger and exhaustion are making them impossibly cranky. And let's be honest, it isn't always easy to shake off our own workday stress and we might be tired, hungry, and cranky ourselves. We've heard a bunch of tips from working moms on how to make the transition from day to evening a bonding experience for everyone.

FEED THEM AND YOURSELF

Snacks on the way home can be a lifesaver. It calms kids down when their appetites are sated. So if you pick up your kids from day care, bring something, or if they are home with the nanny, then make sure they give them something to hold them over. And don't forget to eat a little protein yourself, a piece of cheese or yogurt, anything which will give you energy going into dinnertime.

SET UP A TRANSITION SPACE

A pile of pillows in their room, a chair, anywhere you can spend ten minutes decompressing with your kids. Remember, you are shaking off the day too, so turn off the cell phone and pull out Dr. Seuss.

EAT DINNER TOGETHER

It's not always possible, and let's face it, it's rarely easy to eat at six, but it's a nice way to wind down and reconnect. It's also a time to focus exclusively on the kids, who need some attention from you. So have wine with your spouse later and pasta with your kids now.

HAVE A NIGHTLY RITUAL

We've always heard kids respond well to having a schedule. What is surprising is how quickly a busy working mom will start relying on one too. Knowing exactly what needs to get done helps all of us exhausted parents get through the long list that includes making dinner, eating dinner, cleaning up after dinner, giving a bath, changing into pajamas, reading stories, getting everyone to bed, and wrapping up whatever work you had left.

BE FIRM ABOUT BEDTIME

Stick to a bedtime and a system for keeping the kids in bed. There are whole books on the subject, so all we'll say is this—the sooner they learn to put themselves to sleep, the better it will be for you.

BE AWARE OF BATH TIME

Some children relax after a soak in the tub and some get ramped up. Schedule the bath time around your child's temperament. It took Caitlin and Andrew months to realize that their kids would run around in circles after their lavender-scented bubble bath.

READ TO YOUR CHILDREN

At least one book a night. In just fifteen minutes each night, you can teach your kids to appreciate reading, help develop and nurture their imagination, and rediscover books you loved.

TURN OFF

Turn off the office until your children go down. If you let yourself, you can begin to enjoy the rhythm of bedtime. It's a time to calm down, refocus, and reconnect with your family and disconnect from the demands of clients, employees, and employers. After the kids are down, then dive back in. Most of the women we interviewed reminded us to give the children your attention when you get home from work and turn off the BlackBerry for a few hours. Our friend Stacy Maddox shared this: "When my 'Berry is on, the urge to check in has become too compelling. I know it's a problem when my toddler daughter tells me I need to stop doing my e-mails."

blackberry: is it really mom's best friend?

We can't live without our BlackBerrys. We check them first thing in the morning and lastly before we go to bed. They are never more than an arm's length away. Our rationale is that if we're on top of things at work, then we can be more flexible in how we spend our time. In theory that makes sense. The reality often looks more like working all of the time—especially to our children. Kim's son has asked her to stop looking at the BlackBerry when he's with her, and Caitlin's husband has instituted a no BlackBerry peek during the movies and dinner.

How did it go so wrong so fast? We thought the BlackBerry was the best thing in the world when we first got one. Caitlin's always looking for good news, and Kim is trying to stay one step ahead of the to-do list. Through excessive use, we've created a monster that our families resent, and our clients now expect that we are continuously available. Will Schwalbe, a friend to Girl's Guide and author of *Send: Why People Email So Badly and How to Do It Better* (Knopf, 2008), recommends the following tips to cut down on BlackBerry and e-mail use:

- If you send an e-mail and don't need or want a reply, end it with, "Thanks, no reply necessary."
- If an e-mail volley seems as if it will never end, schedule a phone call to wrap up the issue.
- If you don't want e-mails at all hours of the day and night, don't send or reply to them during those hours. You can actually write up all the replies in advance, just don't send them until an appropriate time.
- When trying to figure out if it's an appropriate time to pull out the BlackBerry, ask yourself if it would be an appropriate time to pull out a *New York Times* crossword puzzle. If the answer is no, then leave the 'Berry in the bag.

girl talk

We interviewed Kelly Winston, a working mom with two daughters, who is one of those people who impresses you with how together she always appears. While we really wanted to ask her how in the world she seems so perfect, we decided that might make her uncomfortable, so we stuck with these questions.

Do you think it is ever possible to strike a perfect balance between being a great mom and great employee?

My generation was taught by our pioneering mothers that we could be anything we wanted to be. But what they forgot to teach us was that we cannot be everything to everyone at the same time. That is our dilemma and the balance left to be discovered by today's women.

Recently, I had a girls' weekend with two friends from college. I work full-time in communications. My friend in California works three days a week for a management-consulting firm, and my friend in Texas just left her public interest job and is now home full-time and expecting her third. The amazing thing was that none of us were exactly sure we were doing the right thing. My California friend has now passed up the opportunity for promotion twice to preserve her wonderful schedule, and while, as a mother, she knows it is the right thing for her and her family, the Type-A side of her still longs to prove herself.

Lately, I've been thinking a lot about choosing what I *should* do versus what I *can* do. I can take on more responsibility, create grand plans and strategies, and execute the heck out of them. But that isn't necessarily what I should do. I'm not living or working just for myself, and expending all my energy and emotional reserves between 8:00 and 6:00 isn't fair to those I committed to long before I committed to this job. So, for me it isn't a matter of striking a balance between being a great mom and a great employee. It's about remembering to balance what I can do and what I should do.

We look at the coverage of celebrity moms with their entourages of nannies and wonder if there are any realistic role models in the media today?

I tend to think of celebrity mothering the same way I think of celebrity weight loss. The magazines splash the headlines "Diet Secrets of the Stars" across the cover, but nowhere in the article does it say that to achieve the same effects you need to hire a personal chef who specializes in Mediterranean fare and a personal trainer who will kick your butt four hours per day. In my opinion, even the "down-to-earth" media stars—Reese Witherspoon, for example, who is one of the few who admits how hard it actually is—live a life so far removed from my own that there is no sense in drawing a comparison.

I know many women who look to their own mothers for inspiration. My neighbor said to me once, "My mom and I fought a lot when I was growing up, but her working was never the reason." My mother was a homemaker and a volunteer, but she has always encouraged me to be true to myself.

I also look to the president of my local liberal arts university, who is a great inspiration to me. When I was a freelancer, we used to be in the same yoga class at 5:00 on Wednesdays. Since returning to the corporate setting full-time, I haven't been once. Recently we exchanged e-mails, and she wrote, "Find time for yoga. Young moms need it the most!"

Any tips you can share for those moms looking for a smoother morning?
When I chose to reenter the corporate workplace, my greatest fear was that my two least favorite times of the day—morning routine and late afternoon—were all I would have left with my own children. It still isn't easy. At times I want to pull out my hair (or theirs). But since it is all I have, I find that I love those hours no matter what.

That being said, here are my tips.

Make yourself get up and finish your own routine before your preschool children awake. As hard as it is when that alarm goes off, I am always glad to have time to focus on them exclusively without trying to remember if I put mascara on both eyes or only one. (By the way, I am terrible at actually following my advice on this one. I love and crave sleep too much to be rational before the sun is up!)

What about a smoother bedtime?
My older daughter (age six) has a responsibility chart in her room that her nanny created. It allows her to check off every step required for going to bed—e.g., go to potty, wash hands, brush teeth, put clothes in hamper. It is such a relief to be able to say simply "Go do your chart," rather than give a separate instruction for each item. We use a kitchen timer and if she gets it all done in twenty

minutes, she gets an extra chapter or song at bedtime. I cannot wait for my younger daughter to get to that point!

Do you and your husband have time alone?
We do. I have a triple life—that is, employee, mother, and wife. Wife is the one that gets neglected most often. Admittedly, I pour out a lot of myself into work. When I get home, I rally and do the same for the kids. But by the time it's just the two of us, I'm spent! Fall is the best season for us, because we have two season tickets to our local NFL games. Most Sundays we have four hours to sit together in the afternoon—when we're both wide awake—and cheer.

We also make it a point not to discuss household business at 9 p.m. When we're both drained, a simple question, "Did you call the tree guy?," can sound like an accusation. And the response often becomes something like this: "No, I didn't call the tree guy. Don't you think, after you've asked me three times, that if I *did* call the tree guy you'd be the first to know?" We try to have breakfast or lunch on neutral territory every other week. We each bring our list of questions and to-dos. Not romantic, but effective!

What do you think the biggest challenges are that first year of working and mothering?
Aside from everything I wrote about above, I still haven't figured out how to feed everyone dinner. I know that sounds ridiculous because there are a lot of solutions out there. One friend cooks after her kids go to bed for herself and her husband. Then the next night, she reheats leftovers for the kids and starts over. I've just never been able to get into that kind of groove. Feeding the children is actually easy. Cut up fruit, steam some veggies, add fish sticks or Bagel Bites and voilà! But that precludes any sort of family meal time, which is important to me. It also means Nick and I stand at the fridge scratching our heads at 8:30, and my father-in-law (who prefers to eat before six) is left to his own devices.

Sometimes I remember to order from Weekday Gourmet so that I have easy meals in the freezer, but then I forget to thaw them out and/or ask my nanny to put them in the oven. My manager thinks I'm a very organized person. He's never been to my house for dinner.

Do you find yourself doing more at home than your husband? If so, any advice for women who are faced with a similar challenge?

Yes. To his credit, he offers and, I believe, legitimately wants to do more. However, he doesn't see what needs to be done as easily as I do or often at all. When I see something, I do it, even if that means picking up after him. It's easier and faster than delegating. (Funny, that's something I constantly work on at the office as well.) I laugh that the work that needs to be done at home is like one court's definition of pornography—I can't define it, but I know it when I see it! Sometimes I'll try to start a list for him, and to his credit he will often make one for himself for the weekends. But his list usually involves projects like install intercom system or blow leaves off roof. My mental list is created and checked off minute-by-minute—bring items left downstairs (including his coat and tie) upstairs, check washer (to make sure the wash he started was moved to the dryer), clean jelly off countertop (from when he made kids' sandwiches) . . .

work at home and home at work

Harried working mothers often forget that many of the skills that make them great employees and bosses could also help them at home. At the same time, aspects of your home life can be carried over and used effectively at the office. We are so busy trying to maintain the boundaries between our professional and personal lives that we may be missing opportunities to make our lives easier.

Nothing, absolutely nothing, will test and hone your patience like having children. We read somewhere that the average child says "Mom" two-hundred-plus times a day. That alone will make you crazy. And how about the numerous times you are interrupted at home? Doesn't it always seem like the time your child is suddenly dying for a snack is when you are trying to finish a paragraph or clean the kitchen? Your child wants as much of your attention as he or she can get, and when you're not exhausted it's the greatest feeling in the world. Unfortunately, for the first couple of years after your baby is born you are exhausted. All of the time.

The good news is that these same factors: the neediness, the lack of control and requisite selflessness can make you a more patient, understanding, and compassionate boss.

There are myriad opportunities to grow alongside your child. Your career is important to you, so take a broad perspective about the challenges you are overcoming at home. Do a little self-examination. If you are fighting for equal housework at home, do you take that spirit into your boss's office when asking for a raise? If you are taking on the bulk of child care on the weekends and declining offers of help from the people around you, are you also stretching yourself too thin at the office? If your spouse has told you that you are too critical of his parenting style, are you micromanaging your team as well?

Beyond the business skills you are developing while parenting, if you step back and look at the dynamics of parenting, you can also see the more philosophical truths that you can bring into work—you can't control everything, you should appreciate the downtime when it comes and realize nothing stays the same. Life is a series of moments.

While the Mom Hat and the Work Hat are different, you are still wearing both—and you are not two people. How can you seamlessly merge your two selves to be a more successful career girl and more fulfilled mother? How can you take what you learn in each world and make a stronger, smarter, happier you? The key is to be engaged in all aspects of your life, giving full focus to what's in front of you at that moment. Don't rush past the challenges or tough conversations, because every one of them is an opportunity for you to get better or become clearer about something. And all of this learning can be applied to all aspects of your life.

In this chapter, you'll find suggestions for how to bring that business-self home to get things a little more streamlined, to delegate effectively, and to apply some of that hard-earned workplace savvy to negotiations for time off over the breakfast table. And you'll also see where some of those things you are learning at home can actually help you at the office.

be an office manager at home

Those of you who are or have a reliable, smart, organized office manager, consider yourself lucky. Office managers clean up the mess and implement the systems you need to do your job. They make it easier for you to buzz through your to-do list because they have taken away the clutter and distractions. Now, we all know that nothing brings clutter and distraction like children. Even those who maintain the most pristine households find themselves picking up LEGOs and graham crackers embedded in the sofa.

Setting up a system for organizing your family will go a long way to helping your life run more smoothly. The systems will be different for everyone, but here are some helpful fundamentals to guide you.

THE WEEKDAY SYSTEM

The key to a smooth week is a reasonable and realistic schedule. All too often we high-achieving women think we can do everything in half the time that it actually takes. Start by writing down the entire family schedule (it doesn't matter how well you think you know it, to create an effective system it needs to be on paper). Start with the times that everyone has to be at their first location. For example, you need to be at work at 9:00 a.m., the kids need to be at the bus stop by 8:15 a.m., and your partner needs to catch a 7:45 a.m. train.

Next, list all the tasks that need to be accomplished to get everyone out the door on time—no task is too small to include. Then keep track of the time these tasks take for a week. You might be surprised by how much time it actually takes to get the kids cleaned, dressed, fed, and packed. And don't forget that you also have to get yourself cleaned and dressed and out the door. To calculate your ideal wakeup time, tally the minutes for each task. Add ten minutes for a cushion and then subtract it from the wake-up times. This will give you your optimum wake-up time.

Once you've got the morning in check, tackle the afternoon. Apply the same process to the "Back in the Door" activities and schedule. Write down everyone's schedule (and this can be tricky, as they frequently change from week to week) and make a plan for coverage. Pickups, play dates, and practices, not to mention after-work responsibilities and family time, are really tough to cover adequately, but seeing it all on paper will help it feel more manageable.

Assign responsibilities to each member of the family—don't forget the children can (and should) be responsible for appropriate tasks.

Next, consider your priorities and don't be afraid to think out of the box to stay in line with them. Sitting down together for a family meal is one of Chrisi Colabella's biggest priorities. But with two daughters who have a daily schedule of sports games, practices, and more than an hour of homework each, sitting down to a formal dinner became an impossible and unpleasant event. Food was rushed, the girls were tired, and the time they shared was neither pleasant nor productive. The mom in Chrisi became sad and frustrated. The manager in her went to work. How could she rearrange the schedule so she and the girls spent positive time around the table? Breakfast time for her was the obvious choice. They are all early risers, and now every morning before school they sit down to "dinner." She cooks the family meals on Sunday because that's the only time she has free, and at night they grab something light—

could be soup or fruit and yogurt—and don't put a lot of pressure around the evening schedule. By 9:00 p.m., everyone, including Chrisi, is exhausted and ready for bed. Five-thirty a.m. comes pretty quickly.

Of course, Chrisi's solution may not work for you, but the lessons are critical. Stay focused on your priorities and keep adjusting the system (and perhaps the schedule) until you find a solution that works for your family.

You have all the information you need now to create the family schedule and accompanying list of individual responsibilities. We recommend you use the same system you use at work. Or if you are separated and sharing custody of your child, consider an online calendar so you can both be on top of the schedule and aware of any changes.

By the time the weekend rolls around we are exhausted. Fight the urge to lay around the house (would if it were possible) and get a few things checked off your list so you can start the week relaxed on Monday.

The weekend system

- Review the week ahead of you with your spouse and make a weekly to-do list.
- Think about the upcoming weekend plans and add confirmed play dates to the weekly to-do list. You don't want to be waking up on a rainy Saturday with nothing planned for rambunctious kids.
- Stick to the school's nap, lunch, and snack schedule whenever possible. It makes it much easier for your preschooler to transition between home and school when the schedule is the same.
- Pay the bills.
- Commit to giving yourselves some time together (date night?)

and some time alone (yoga studio?) and fit that into the schedule of every weekend.

Shopping

- Plan meals ahead of time. It really helps to know what your dinner options are when you are exhausted.
- Include a few frozen meals in there, and these days there are loads of guilt-free options (Amy's makes great pizzas).
- When shopping, there are certain things you will always need. Buy the following items in bulk to avoid last-minute trips to the store: Neosporin, Band-Aids, diaper cream, baby shampoo, onesies, T-shirts, socks (because they disappear, even in your own washer/dryer), juice boxes, and every snack known to woman. Caitlin and Andrew can't believe how much their kids can eat.

It might seem overwhelming at first to have to create and follow any system when you are already feeling like every day is crunch time but, believe us, just like a well-run office when you remove the clutter, you can just focus on enjoying your children.

negotiating tactics that might just work at home

We'll deal with this more in Chapter Seven (because never is negotiation more important than in dealing with one's partner), but negotiating is one of the key work skills that you can bring home. You've realized by now that you can't do it all, that work responsibilities are nipping at your heels as you run out the door to pick up your kid from day care. That this time you absolutely can't avoid the business trip. That you need to start exercising before you leave for work. Whatever it is you need today, you will also need something tomorrow, next week, and six months from now. Because of the inflexibility of time in your child's schedule, you and your partner are the ones who need to adjust. The only wiggle room you have is what the other gives you, so get your negotiation face on.

The good news is that you are Ms. Career woman, and you have likely gotten a raise, promotion, or a coveted project utilizing the very skills that are going to make your life easier at home. And remember, we as women are more likely to say yes without putting our partner through the same hoops so make sure you are walking away with something—even if it's a morning to sleep in—if you are asked to do significantly more on the home front. Now, in an ideal world, all of us would just do whatever our partner needed without fuss, but let's get real. We are tired and burnt out and neither of us have a lot of extra energy to give. So let's start with having some compassion for each other's situation, but don't let it get in the way of asking for what you need.

the word

A COUPLE OF THOUGHTS FROM THE TOP OF THE LADDER

Lisa M. Weber is the president of Individual Business at MetLife, Inc., and the mother of two children. We have always maintained that the view is much different from the highest rungs of the ladder, and in an interview for the Forte Foundation Web site Lisa shares two important pieces of advice that can help us all:

High-ranking executive women should *not* try to achieve work-life balance. According to Lisa, "People struggle so much with the word *balance*. Give it up. There is no such thing as balance. It is about prioritization. If you want balance, you cannot be in these jobs. I know that's very disappointing for some, but you cannot be the president of a business and work from home three days a week when you have 20,000 people running around the country."

With two school-age children, Lisa rises at 4 a.m. on the weekends so that she can work before her children wake up. She clears her calendar for special or one-time events, like the installation of her son's braces, the first day of school, their departure to summer camp, and extended family vacations, but she prioritizes her work to ensure that high-level matters are addressed and completed as well.

When your life is in "family mode," be a good role model. When Lisa gave birth to her first child, a son, she stayed home for five weeks. "He was a preemie and in the hospital for three of the five weeks," she recalls. "And going back to work so fast was a huge mistake . . . not only from the standpoint of me not being able to spend that time and bond with my son, but also in not being the role model that I believe I am for other women." After the birth of her daughter, Lisa stayed home for three months. She offers unsolicited advice to others urging them to do what is right for their situation.

running an effective meeting for your staff and your family

Put on your office hat for a second. Meetings are effective when the parties come prepared and fully focused. We dread most meetings because they are a waste of time. Usually, the only thing actually agreed to is when to have the next meeting. If the manager comes to the meeting with a specific list of items to address, delegates tasks, is provided with updates and recaps next steps, then it's a successful meeting.

Think about how many details you are juggling at home. During any given month you could be planning a birthday party or buying gifts for someone else's, scheduling a business trip, buying new clothes because your baby had a growth spurt, trying to accommodate your nanny's request for a week off, taking the dog to the vet, negotiating for nighttime coverage thanks to a big project at work, trying to get a run in at least a few times a week, finding a painter for the house, taking the car in for a tune-up, researching local day care centers. Wow. That is a whole lotta stuff going on and we're guessing your list for next month is even longer. It seems like it's in your family's best interest for you to set up a family meeting to start delegating and figure out if maybe you need another set of hands for some of it.

As we know, the best way to handle a meeting is to come prepared. So write down everything that needs to get done this month—both the household jobs and everything about your work that could be impacting your personal time. That includes any commitments that will require skipping a morning or evening with your child. Write down any scheduling issues your school or nanny has brought up. Remember to include any doctor's appointments and car and pet care. Now, factor in any personal time you want to get in there and need to discuss.

Ideally, you each will come to the meeting with your list because your partner will have his job responsibilities and requests for personal time to add to the mix. He may also be aware of household tasks that you forgot (yes, it's true . . . you don't know everything) to include.

To keep the meeting focused, try to schedule it at a time when you are conscious. That would mean Friday night is most likely out, as is the crack of dawn on Monday. We spoke to several women who find time during the week for a breakfast or lunch with their spouses to get through the to-do list outside of the chaos of the household.

respectfully delegating child care

Delegation, of course, is another area to put your brilliant professional skills to work at home. When you are a working mom you will find yourself telling a nanny, preschool teacher, or teenage babysitter what to do and how to do it. So put on your boss hat and delegate with respect. Be clear about your expectations when you tell someone what to do. Give them the tools they need to get the job done and set them up for success. If you hire a babysitter for the night, make sure he has your contact numbers and emergency information. Give him a tour of the house and show him where all of the supplies are stored. Walk him through the evening's schedule and fill him in on the temperament of your child. The more information you give the people jumping in to care for your child, the better.

If the providers are not doing things the way you would like—too little time outside, feeding them too many sweets—instead of blowing up, double check to see if you have given them what they need to do the job the way you expect. If the nanny isn't taking your child out enough during the day, find out if she is at a loss for where to go or if she is concerned about the temperature outside. If she is feeding them sweets, is there a shortage of healthy snacks in the fridge? Good delegating, like anything else, relies on good communication. So before yelling at your child care providers, apply your professional problem-solving skills and figure out the root of the problem.

And accept the fact that you can't do everything yourself. Working mother and Internet professional Lori Greene reminds us that "Working mothers need to delegate, delegate, delegate. Your children should do chores and work around the house. You should share the load with your husband—because if you take it all on yourself, you only have yourself to blame when you're doing 85 percent of everything. Try to start off on the right foot about sharing responsibilities and *let go of control*. Nobody will do it exactly like you and you need to accept that."

drawing boundaries

Drawing that boundary between work and home is impossible these days, especially for working moms who are tethered to their Black-Berry. Working mother Maria Morris agrees: "I'm always accessible and can work anytime, but I have learned to turn off the computer once the kids are home as I'm not good to anyone when doing both. If I want to clear some e-mails, I'll wait until they're in bed because it will only take a half hour and I won't be screaming at anyone!"

Not screaming is always good and, in reality, if you are trying to work while parenting you aren't doing a great job in either camp. It's also a fast track to total burnout if you can't ever focus on one thing. That headache you get after putting your kids down could be due in part to the fact that you were e-mailing while boiling pasta water and answering to both "Mommy!" and "Honey!" Kim Parrish, creator and founder of the Kim Parrish Collection, shares this: "I used to live by the philosophy, 'Work Hard, Play Hard.' But after Chase was born we realized we would need to alter our definition of playing to include blocks, toy cars, and pop-up books. Finding balance has been quite a challenge. Craig and I both enjoy the hurdles associated with achieving goals, growing businesses, launching product lines, and networking our resources. We've had to become creative in finding the hours in a day needed to finish projects without pulling time or attention away from Chase. It's not unusual that we'll leave the office at 5 p.m. only to return to 'work mode' at 8 p.m. once Chase is tucked into bed so we can finish a project."

No one should feel like they have to put away the ambition once they become a mother. We have all worked too hard on ourselves and our careers to toss either away. But there is a way to structure the day so you are not killing yourself trying to do everything at the same time. Burnout is real. It makes you tired, irritable, unable to concentrate and motivate. It leads to short tempers, late projects, and a seriously compromised quality of life. What you need to do now as a working mom is to prioritize everything and everyone. That includes your children, friendships, relationships with family members, travel, business projects, vacations, goals, and, not least of all, your romantic life. The upshot of every major change in your life is as something goes away, another takes its place. You have a new kind of emotionally rich life when you become a parent and, along with that, your free time and wiggle room has gone out the window.

Enter each day knowing you are going to do your best and give what you can give. Since people (your boss, child, spouse) won't be setting boundaries for you, it's up to you.

On the work front decide how available you want to be to your employer and/or employees and clients when you are not in the office. Think carefully about the projects you take on, the business travel you commit to. On the home front make sure the household tasks are assigned evenly, and don't volunteer for too much. Maria Morris adds, "Keep the activities that add to your entire family's well-being, not just your child's. If your entire family is paying the price for the activity, is it worth it? My favorite activity is soccer practice as I get to sit down with a cold drink and chat with the other moms while my kid is running around. I get to chill for an hour! Pure bliss!!!"

be open to advice (some of it may just work)

You routinely collaborate with coworkers and seek the suggestions and support of your boss and mentor at work; use the same tools in your home life. Seek out advice and be open to even the unsolicited sort. Your abrasive mother-in-law, the busybody on line in front of you at the supermarket, your best friend with triplets, or your client who happens to be a single mother—all of these women could have advice that helps you figure out this working-mom thing. We know, it's hard to hear advice from people you may find annoying or have complicated relationships with, but when you are both mothers, things change. Seriously, they do. You now have something profound in common. The responsibility for another human being. And those of us who have that responsibility plus are still ambitious and engaged in our careers, we have even more in common. Be open to advice from the working mothers around you and don't be afraid to ask them questions.

A FEW HELPFUL QUESTIONS TO ASK OTHER WORKING MOMS

- What is your morning schedule?
- How do you deal with the guilt of seeing your child crying when you drop off at day care?
- How do you find time for yourself?
- What do you do if you find yourself doing all of the housework and most of the child care?
- How late do your kids stay up and what is the nighttime routine?
- What do you do if your kids just don't stay in bed?
- When do you think it would be okay for me to go on a business trip?
- Do you feel like your boss is unsupportive of your role as working mother?
- Did you feel like your coworkers made assumptions about you and your work when you got back from maternity leave?

don't micromanage your team or your partner

If you want your partner more engaged in taking care of the kids or the housework, then please, let them do it their way. Nothing is more debilitating and annoying than having someone over your shoulder telling you how to fill the dishwasher the "right" way. Over the summer, Kim was staying with friends who have a four-year-old daughter. One afternoon the husband took the daughter for a stroll into town to the library. It was a short trip, but instead of spending the thirty minutes relaxing, the wife complained to Kim about how she was sure he forgot to pack a snack "because he always does" and how he never changes her into sneakers. And most of all how frustrated she was that he didn't do more. Didn't do more?! Would you?

Kim Parrish says, "Of course I micromanaged at first! Luckily, my husband is a strong, loving, kind man who realizes his wife has the best interest of the family in mind. When we first had Chase I barked out orders better than any drill sergeant. I've since learned to realize I need to relax and trust in Craig's parenting skills. He may do things differently, but there are no set rules to proper parenting and Chase benefits from the variety."

When we wrote our second book, *The Girl's Guide to Being a Boss Without Being a Bitch*, we interviewed 150 women on various aspects of leadership. We asked a few of the very well-respected managers how they got the best work from their employees. They said, most of all, let them do their job. If you micromanage, they will eventually give up and leave everything for you to do. It's true. When you constantly correct someone on the job they are doing, you are undermining their self-confidence. And only self-confident people take on more. So if you want your partner to do more, start with appreciating the bit he does now. Believe us; you don't want to become Kim's friend who is heading for zero help from her husband.

Your chance to get this started on the right foot at the beginning is to let your partner spend time with your baby solo. There is a myth that women are born with all the answers when it comes to how to take care of an infant. We are so committed to this untruth that we are often hesitant to ask for advice and are offended if people step in to guide us. But why should we know everything about babies? Most of us are learning on the job, so let your partner figure things out too. If you let him find his way into parenting on his own, then he will have the confidence to take care of the baby without you (a gift six months down the road when you have a work crisis or just need a break). If, however, you are criticizing his methods of child care, won't leave him alone with the baby, and jump in to take over the minute there is a cry, then you are setting patterns that will bite you down the road when you are ready for more autonomy.

the word

ADVICE FROM ONE WORKING MOTHER

Caitlin was working with Amy Shanler from Staples on a few projects. It turned out they both had twins, and lucky for Caitlin, Amy's were six months older. Over the course of the next several months, Amy was kind enough to share her tips for transitioning from cribs to toddler beds, ideas about meal planning and morning schedules. She was so generous with her time and experience that it actually made those early years of parenting twins easier for Caitlin. Here were some of the questions she asked Amy:

What was it like for you coming back to work after having the twins?

I feel like I had two back-to-work transitions. Actually, three. When the kids were born, I had plans of returning to my previous job at a PR agency. However, the more time I spent with them and balancing the demands of my role and the cost to keep both babies in day care full-time, I knew something had to give. So my first return back after maternity leave was a visit to my current employer to give my notice. That went a lot better than I thought. People were happy to see me and the babies, and understood the economics of my situation. All was good, but I felt a sense of sadness as I cleaned out my office. I still consider that *my* office even though someone else had moved in.

Then I had the start of my job as executive director of the Publicity Club. For my first professional meeting, I brought the babies. There's nothing like taking notes on your assignments, roles, and responsibilities while feeding two babies bottles. This job brought the joys of working out of the house, with a few events per month where I would leave the kids with a sitter. It was a good balance. However, the taste of working and responsibility left me wanting more (and truthfully, I was a little bored with Mother Goose and *Pat the Bunny*). Plus, I was working so hard, taking care of kids during the day and on the laptop until quite late. Frankly, I didn't have a lot of time for my husband and figured I could achieve greater balance if I went back to work full-time.

So on to my first full-time position after the babies were born. Honestly, I had the easiest transition, in part because my kids were fifteen months old, and in part because my boss is one of the greatest, most understanding souls in the world. He is a father of four, values my work (he was my client while I was at the PR agency), and saw me working so hard and delivering results that he understood when I needed to pick up the kids and run them to the doctor.

The biggest surprise was that I was happy. This happiness spread beyond work into my home life. I was glad to see my kids because I missed them. We had fun when we were together. I was able to leave work at work, or tend to anything I had to put on hold after the kids were in bed. I saw my husband and we were able to catch up on life. Work for me is good.

What were you going through emotionally those first few months? Were you questioning your choices?

My kids got so much more out of day care in the first week than I could have given them in a month. On day two, the teacher said, "You don't paint with them at home, do you?" Um, paint? "No." "Yeah, we could tell." I thought to myself: Are you going to come to my house to clean it up? All kidding aside, the talented caregivers at our day care have much more creativity and experience stimulating children than I do. I recognized this early on and this helped increase my comfort level in their situation.

Do you wish you had handled things differently in any way?

I really overcompensated when I had to be out of the office for my kids—on the BlackBerry in the doctor's waiting room or conducting conference calls on the way to CVS. I eventually learned the work will still be there. If my kids really need me, I really need to be there for them—fully there, not half in my e-mail. I did figure this out and no real harm done, but it's something I wish I learned earlier.

What did you learn from the working moms around you?

It all comes down to priorities and perspective. At the end of the day, what is the most important thing? And what is the worst that can happen if . . . The answers to those questions keep things real. They also had support and were not afraid to use it. My teammate has her mom living with her; the boss's boss has a nanny. And that is okay. Just because you have help doesn't stop you from being the mom.

Did you feel at any point that you were being judged by your coworkers or treated differently?

I am not sure of anything I felt overtly—it was more the internal angst I felt when I walked in at 9:10 and imagined I felt people hush. Or when I needed to leave at 5:00 and asked a teammate to do the 5–5:30 meeting for me. She never said anything about it, but I imagine there were comments made. I overcompensate, though—and feel like I need to clear my in-box before work the next day. If

I can't work a "normal" work day, I'll show them I can still keep up my work and even do better.

girl talk

SUSAN BURSK

Susan Bursk is a third-generation working mother. Her grandparents owned several restaurants together and her parents opened a hardware store and worked together six days a week. She shares with us what it was like to have a working mother at a time when it was highly unusual.

Tell us what it was like for you to be one of the only kids with a mom at work?
My mom approached everything with such a positive attitude. She made me feel as though I was very special and lucky to be the only child in grammar school who went to an after-school day camp. I remember I would always volunteer my mother to do things at school...i.e., bake cakes for the May Festival. Sometimes she would say, "Aren't there any other mothers to bake a cake?" But she never let me down. She was always there for me whenever I asked her to do something for my school. I think it was my way of knowing that when I needed her, she could be counted on...and she never made me feel guilty about it.

Were you jealous of the other kids?
While other moms wore dresses, mine wore pants. For me, growing up with a working mom and grandmother was the way it was. I asked one of my closest friends if I ever said anything to her about my mom always working. She said, "Everyone knew your parents had a business and worked. It was just the way it was."

What changes did you make when you became a working mom based on how you were raised?

My mom was always available for me and I wanted to be sure my son knew I was always available for him. However, what I came to realize was what I needed from my mom, my son did not necessarily need from me. I spoke to my mom every day on the phone. Literally every day until the day she died. Although my son and I have a close relationship, we don't have that same need for daily contact. We are different people, with different needs and expectations. While I recognize our similarities, more important, I recognize our differences and embrace them.

Do you have any advice for women in that first tough year of being a working mom?
In general, I believe women tend to do it all—taking care of the house, the bills, the marketing, making meals for the family, and working full/part-time on top of all that. I think it's important to recognize that we are not superhuman and that's okay. Paying attention to what is considered realistic expectations is the first step to alleviating guilt. Asking for help is the second step. And the third step is getting help, whether it's from family, friends, or a nanny or housekeeper. Whatever you need to do to make it work and lessen the feeling of "I need to do it all."

a partnership that works

Ask any working mother who does more at home and the answer will be the mother. Can all of us working mothers possibly be martyrs, or worse, delusional? Unfortunately, no. The sad truth is that women shoulder the majority of responsibilities on the home front even if they also contribute to the family financially. Most families need two working parents to survive, so how come every time I come home from work, my children ask me what's for dinner even though my husband has been home for two hours?

We think it's time for a change and, unfortunately, change takes time. Don't be discouraged when you try out our recommendations on your spouse and you are met with nothing resembling enthusiasm. Don't give in because "it's just easier to do it yourself." This chapter will arm you with the tools you need to create a better working family partnership. Your children will be happier if you and your partner are working as a team. You will be happier if you and your partner are working as a team.

Read this chapter and follow its advice. This may be the most important chapter in the book, because if your partnership is solid, then your children can thrive and you two can love and respect each other and maybe even have a little fun together facing the challenges that raising kids in this century brings.

just because you can doesn't mean you should

We keep hearing the same frustration voiced in our interviews. "Why can't my spouse do as much as I can?" We don't need studies to show us that working mothers shoulder significantly more of the responsibilities at home (although there are many to cite). Men wouldn't even argue the point. We then ask the question, "Why aren't you demanding more support from your partner?" The answers have been either "I am the mother so it's my responsibility" or "It's just easier if I do it myself."

Just because you gave birth to the child does not mean it's solely your responsibility to take care of him. It takes a village to raise a child and, in absence of one, you had better force your partner to share in the responsibility. Standing up for yourself is not just a matter of trying to achieve fairness and equality. Standing up for yourself will save you hours of anger and frustration. Women who feel overburdened for too long report feelings of anger and resentment toward their spouses. The spouses report they are taken by surprise by the level and intensity of their partner's anger. You can see how resentment, anger, and surprise can cause problems for a marriage. And when there are problems in a marriage, you suffer, your spouse suffers, your child suffers, and your job suffers.

Of course it is easier to just do it yourself—and you *can* probably do it better too. But you need to delegate (just like your boss explained in your last review). You have too many things on your plate and if you don't get them off, you will be crushed. If your spouse is already maxed out, then try to find a way to get help from a relative, or if you can afford it, hire someone to walk the dog, mow the lawn, clean the house, or any task that you and your spouse continually argue about.

the word

THE RIGHT PARTNER MAKES ALL THE DIFFERENCE

Eileen Moore Andersen earned her M.B.A. from Emory University and is a regional controller working for General Mills in a joint venture with Nestlé. She's the mother of two girls and her husband is a stay-at-home dad named Dave.

Eileen and Dave's passion is travel. They met while they were studying abroad in Austria during college and got married shortly after they graduated. Eileen followed Dave to Atlanta, where he was doing graduate work at Emory. To pay the bills she got a temporary clerical job at Coca-Cola. She was ultimately hired full-time, and she and Dave decided that international travel was their goal and getting there through her job was the easiest route.

While Dave was working on his Ph.D., Eileen was accepted into Emory's evening M.B.A. program. It was a total grind and they rarely saw each other, but they were in no rush to have children and an M.B.A. would open the doors they needed to get overseas.

After Eileen graduated, she got accepted into the MBA Enterprise Corp., which is an NGO that sends M.B.A.s to developing countries where they work in different companies creating business plans and helping them grow. Eileen and Dave were off to Ukraine in 1997 for a fifteen-month assignment, including a ten-week home study learning the local language. This was not a big bucks job. Eileen was paid $900 a month and lodging for her and her husband.

During the Ukraine placement Eileen worked for small and medium enterprises, including a glass factory and a fish farm where she helped them write business plans. She ended up staying for two years because the NGO she was volunteering for, Alliance for Enterprise Development, hired her. During that time, Dave did all sorts of little jobs. He taught freshman literature at an English language university and he edited an online news daily translating Ukrainian into English.

When she returned to the States in the summer of 2000, the economy was booming, so Eileen was able to be patient and look for a multinational company that would be in line with their longer-term goals. They chose to settle in Minneapolis, as it was Dave's hometown and there were a number of multinational companies for Eileen to apply to. That summer they lived off credit cards and Dave's tips from his barista job at Caribou Coffee.

Three months after being back, Eileen landed a job at Pillsbury (Pillsbury was acquired by General Mills in 2001) and Dave started teaching at the University of Wisconsin–River Falls. Their daughter Rosie was born in July 2002. Bridget was born in 2004 and when she was four months old they were transferred to Albuquerque (a means to the end of getting overseas). In June 2007, Eileen and her family finally got their overseas placement. They were off to Chile on a three-year contract.

Their hope is to get one more three-year overseas contract and then return to the States. Their girls will be ready to put down roots, and Dave and Eileen's parents will be in their eighties. Dave and Eileen want their girls to experience the world and she is very proud that they've accomplished it. The girls are fluent in Spanish and already understand that when it's winter in Chile, it's summer in the United States. Eileen's not sure she understood that until she was an adult.

Eileen credits her family's success to Dave (and we would guess he would say the same about her). Their priorities and goals have always been aligned (travel and adventure) and they've always acted as a team. He's been a stay-at-home dad since the girls were born.

Eileen shares some thoughts about juggling work and family and working internationally:

- If you want to work internationally, you need to have patience and be true to your mission. It took me seven years to get us to Chile, and during those seven years I just kept telling anyone who would listen that I wanted to work internationally. It is very expensive for a company to send an employee overseas and they need to be sure it will work out. Our experience in Ukraine really helped to give my company the confidence that I would be able to handle the challenges and stresses unique to life abroad. Be wary: Sometimes your company will offer you things that won't quite fit with the long-term goal. It's tempting to take these jobs out of company loyalty and it's hard to say no (or in other words, tempting to say yes—the path of least resistance). The challenge comes in working with your company to fill their needs while at the same time tapping into your talents and passions.
- To solve the work-balance mystery I say this: Choose your spouse carefully and find a company that pays more than just lip service to work-life balance. I put a barrier between my work life and my private life. I may be here until 8:00 p.m., but I never work on weekends.
- When I was trying to balance work and graduate school, I thought I would be constantly juggling the balls between them. What I learned is that there weren't three balls in the air. There was only the ball that I was holding. When I put down the work ball, I can pick up the family ball.
- The big factor that allows me to have one ball at a time is Dave. Having his support, and knowing that he is home holding the family ball, allows me to be fully in the moment. We choose quality time over quantity time and lifestyle over money. We've made these decisions together and we're a team. I just want to add, although I know I'm lucky to have met David, pure luck hasn't

gotten me where I am. Choices, clarity of mission, and perseverance are the defining factors. When I tell people that I backpacked through Central America for five months, sometimes they say "Oh, you're so lucky to have done that." My response is always "What's stopping you?" I will admit to being lucky that I grew up in a developed country where women are equals (more or less—in the global sense!) and I had parents who loved me and valued education and had the means and willingness to educate me. But the fact that I was in Central America for five months meant I took a risk, rejected stability, quit a job, and sacrificed a "climb up the ladder" to pursue what gave me joy. I'm proud of the choices I've made, but they haven't come without sacrifice.

stay-at-home dads: are they the answer?

A stay-at-home dad sounds like an ideal situation if you can afford it. Who doesn't want a wife? Who wouldn't be thrilled to have someone at home taking care of the children, the house, and you? Be careful what you wish for. Stay-at-home dads are not wives and women are reluctant to give them carte blanche at home the way men typically do with their wives. "My husband has been a stay-at-home dad since our daughters were born. I guess I feel like I am cheating because I don't have the stresses that other working moms do. But I admit that I probably do more than most at-work fathers do too," said Eileen Moore Anderson, a financial analyst.

According to the U.S. census, there were 159,000 stay-at-home dads versus 5,646,000 stay-at-home mothers in 2006. The census defines them as married fathers with children younger than fifteen who have remained out of the labor force for more than one year primarily so they can care for the family while their wives work outside the home. They don't count fathers with part-time jobs or other income. According to the At-Home Dad Newsletter (http://www.angel fire.com/zine2/athomedad), if you include all the fathers who are also in school, retired, and working part-time, the number would be closer to one million.

No matter how you do the math, stay-at-home dads are still a significant minority and they face challenges and stresses that stay-at-home mothers don't. The biggest one may be the attitudes of their wives. Both Kim and Penelope Trunk believe that their marriages failed in part because their husbands chose to stay at home with their children. "I don't think many of these guys are actually choosing to stay at home. Their careers had either stalled or never gotten going, and they figured why not stay home with kids and work on some other projects," said Penelope Trunk. Kim said that she was constantly frustrated by how her husband managed the family. Her house was spotless and her son was loved and well attended to, but that wasn't enough for her. She wanted her husband to be super mom replacing her: scheduling play dates, volunteering at the school, and doing it exactly the way she would have done it if she had chosen to stay home instead. Not only is that unrealistic, it's unfair and a trap that many women fall into.

The stress on the stay-at-home dad is taking a toll on more than their marriages. Researchers conducting a study for the National Institutes for Health in Framingham, Massachusetts, found that men who have been stay-at-home dads most of their adult lives have an 82 percent higher risk of death from heart disease than men who work outside the home. An 82 percent higher risk of dying because they chose to stay home! Worse, the inverse is also true: The study also found that women in high-demand jobs—compared with women in low-authority jobs—have a three times greater risk of heart disease.

Researchers speculate that the role reversal is actually behind the statistics. Bucking society's conventions is stressful, so if you are going to try this route, you need to be very supportive of each other. Apparently it's a matter of life and death.

HERE ARE SOME WAYS TO MAKE A STAY-AT-HOME-DAD SITUATION WORK

- Set expectations together for how the household will run. Your husband is not your employee and needs to be a partner in all decision-making. He is running the household now; once you agree to a plan, you need to let him be in charge.
- Make sure that staying home with the kids is more than a default position. He has to want to take care of the children and home. This is no easy job, not only because child care is exhausting but also because the role reversal can take its toll, too.
- Stay involved with what's going on but don't micromanage. If you want to be part of the meetings with the teacher, then let your husband know to check your calendar before scheduling any meetings. Don't be the scheduler because it's just easier than communicating your schedule.
- Set a system for communicating what's going on at home and for you at work. Make time for each other outside the family.
- Give your husband lots of positive reinforcement and keep your criticisms to yourself.
- Just because you earn it doesn't make it *your* money. This is a family decision and therefore all assets belong to the family.
- Whenever you're frustrated, and there will be numerous times, do a role reversal in your head. If you were the stay-at-home parent, how would you want to be treated?

the word

Miles Hill, a writer and stay-at-home dad, talks to us about parenting and balance, and offers a few suggestions for making it work when you are taking the unconventional route:

Did you leave a career to raise your children?
I was an ink-stained wretch slaving away at home before and after the stork arrived, although post-stork my slaving time took a major hit. In our case, my wife, a chef, usually works afternoons and nights, which means I've been the one to make dinner, read, get everybody off to bed. The exceptions to this were the first four months of our son's life, when my wife was often up breast-feeding. Many couples can trade off when the working parent gets home. In our case that's almost never been feasible.

How was it decided that it was going to be you at home?
Sometimes who stays home is decided *for* rather than *by* you. We couldn't afford for my wife to stay home. A couple of months after our son was born my wife was offered a position as chef of a popular upscale restaurant. The bacon she was bringing home would increase by 50 percent. Oh sure, we'll turn it down. In retrospect, I can't believe we didn't talk more about this. On the other hand, my wife's career might not be what it is today if we had.

What about your writing career?
As each of our kids has grown, they've required less hands-on time, which meant that I had time to write. We still needed a parent at home, but that dovetailed with my desire to always be working on something. Our kids have benefited, but I've also benefited. When we made the decision for me to stay home we didn't know that my wife would remain the primary breadwinner for most of our family life. That hasn't always been easy. When people make assumptions about what my life has been like, they assume I've made a sacrifice. I don't see it that way. From my perspective it's my wife who's made the sacrifice. At times both of us have wished that we could

switch roles without an incredible financial penalty. The hero of this story isn't the dad who gives up everything to stay at home. The hero is my wife, who gave up a lot of family life to support us.

You have taken the unconventional path and people are often uncomfortable (and closeminded) with that. Has socializing been awkward at any point?

There have been a few times when people found out I was the guy on home watch and after following it up with "So, are you getting anything done?" (Yeah, actually, I'm raising my kids), then mysteriously sighted someone across the room they needed to see *right now*, afraid I was going to start blathering about diapers or whether our preschool endorsed Whole Language, I suppose. Thank God most of our friends have been unconventional—artists or restaurant people or independent operators of one stripe or another. The really unexpected thing was how many women wanted to chat me up whenever I was out walking around with my two-year-old in a backpack. On weekend visits to parks and playgrounds with my wife, all of these moms and nannies would look up and say "Hi, how's it going?" and my wife would give me one of her raised-eyebrow *and-who's-that?* looks.

Have you enjoyed this time in your life?

I'm the kind of ham who was born to read aloud to his kids—creating character voices, imitating sound effects, the whole tootling calliope. And my kids ate it up. I loved that intimacy of being inside a story together. Most dads barely get to kiss their young kids good-night. And now that our older one has left for college I'm even more appreciative of my good fortune. I don't suppose there's any way to empirically parse this, but I also have a sense that our kids are more evenly ballasted because they had a dad at home. They'll throw a line to either me or their mom.

Okay, a few other realities. I've had moments when I looked in the mirror and saw a mad person staring back—*What could I have been thinking! My mind's turning to mush! If I don't start talking to more adults I'm going to go insane.* My wife's career has eclipsed my own, such as it is. During my time at home, I've ghosted several books, written a cookbook with her, and just finished the draft of a novel. But does it put us on a career par? Let's just say the Food Network isn't likely to call anytime soon for my recipe for Shrimp Risotto. On the other hand, she's missed out on some of the pleasures of walking alongside Will and Lyra in *The Golden Compass* or the satisfactions of building a LEGO "setup" on the living room carpet. I think missing those moments is harder on women than on men. (Okay, if that's sexist, so be it.) Men seem to paper over ordinary reality with a kind of noise to remind themselves that they're there and only wake up to what they missed years later. My father, a sales manager, was frequently on the road, leaving my brothers and me alone with our mother in rural Michigan for a week at a time. He once confessed how much seeing me interact with our son and daughter pained him, made him realize how much he'd missed.

Slightly off topic, I think I've been a better dad than a writer. Whether that's good or bad I can't say, but I wouldn't trade one for the other.

What would you say to couples who are considering this route but may be apprehensive?

I would encourage them to ask themselves why are you nervous about this option? If saying the phrase *My husband's at home with the kids* makes you see lights floating at the edge of your vision or your stomach do a tarantella, then maybe you ought to reconsider. Nothing's more effective at revealing a partiality to traditional gender roles than trying to mess with them. Not everybody has to be a pioneer. Talk about it and keep talking. (I wish I'd done more of this.) Talk about who will handle what, and when. Nothing has to be set in stone, but believe me, if you both have different expectations about how the operation will work, it's better to find out now instead of trying to negotiate your way out of a 4:30 a.m. conflict. Talk about the future. How long do you envision the arrangement lasting? Until the kids are in school? Longer? Does your spouse have the kind of career that can be put on hold and then picked up in three, five, ten years? How will you feel about being the primary breadwinner? How does your spouse feel about that? Any arrangement is going to chafe at some time or another, and if you don't talk about it you're dead. I can't say it enough: Talk.

plenty of sunshine and water daily:
how to cultivate a good partner

In the words of Aretha Franklin, R-E-S-P-E-C-T, respect, and more than just a little bit. Good partnerships come from shared values and great communication and an underlying respect for the other person's contribution to the parenting. Wow. That sounds simple. And it is on paper. In the real world of sleep deprivation, money stresses, sick children, and cranky employers, finding time for great communication seems like a pipe dream. You need to make it a priority.

The only way to juggle the schedules, handle the unexpected, and otherwise get along is to be flexible, supportive of each other, and occasionally selfless, and find time to talk things over. Working mothers never feel like their partners understand their challenges. Working fathers all too often think that earning money for their family covers their contribution. Sorry. It's 2009 now. We're on an equal playing field and working fathers need to share in the child care in the same way that working mothers do. Here's a couple of tips that can help you open the lines of communication:

- Schedule and keep a weekly meeting during which you review schedules, problems, successes, and new ideas for how the family can operate more efficiently.
- Don't assume because your partner does it differently than you would, that you would do it better. Different is not a value judgment. It's just different.
- Praise each other for a job well done. (Management 101)
- Address problems immediately. Don't grit your teeth and bear it. You will just react inappropriately when the straw breaks the camel's back and do great damage to your cause of equality.

- Set goals together—financial goals are key. Are you savers or spenders? Do you want to try to earn more money or just spend less to cover the additional expense of the children? Fighting over money is very common. And take it from Kim, once you start it's very difficult to stop!
- Give each other a break. You're both learning at this. Isn't it more fun to learn together?

negotiating with your partner

You've been working really hard to cultivate a strong partnership, but you still feel like there is an inequality in the workload and you need to find a way to approach the problem fairly. Once again, your business-girl training kicks in. Why not just negotiate? Give a little to get a little. We've included a little primer on negotiation:

You can't always get what you want . . . but you can negotiate.
- The key to any successful negotiation is that both parties walk away feeling like they won something. So make sure when you begin the discussion you are ready to listen to what your partner wants and give something back too.
- Walk into a negotiation with a plan. Know what you want and be specific. If you want your partner to cover Tuesday and Thursday nights so you can take a class, then ask for that. If you want every other Saturday morning to play tennis, then that's the "ask."
- Do your research. In this arena it would be: How much do you do today? What have they asked for recently? If you "win" this negotiation, then are things out-of-balance at home? What would you need to do to get it back?

- Think and ask big. If you have already sold yourself out at the beginning of the negotiation, then you have no wiggle room. So, make sure you go in high and be willing to come down.

- Make a commitment to yourself to hold your ground. You will not believe what some people will sink to in order to not take on more at home. The guilt trips, the sulking, the attempt to change the agreement. Stand strong. Just like at the office, you have to be your own advocate. If you know what you want, that you deserve it or need it, then *ask* for it.

- Be willing to give something. You can always begin the discussion with your offer and then tackle your ask. That sets a positive tone and your partner might be more receptive to what you are asking for.

the word

LINDA BRIERTY, THERAPIST

Can you share some tips with our readers on how to negotiate more help at home, since so many of us do too much on that front?

Finding balance and a sense of equality on the domestic side of things is a major challenge for most families. The primary breadwinner often feels overwhelmed by financial responsibility, and the partner more in charge of the home front often feels isolated, abandoned, and alone. Obviously, in single parent households this is exacerbated. In families with two breadwinners, it would be nice if domestic duties were divided evenly, but how often does this happen? There is usually a primary parent, largely responsible for the day-to-day running of the home. To avoid resentment, it is helpful to break down responsibilities and agree about who is responsible for what. Be careful not to enable and "pick up the slack" if one partner is not meeting their end of the bargain. Divide responsibilities by identifying each other's strengths, and make sure you agree with each other and feel that it is equitable. Then the agreement must be maintained. Have a weekly "check-in" about how things are going. Try to avoid a victim mentality—if your needs are not being met, it is up to you to communicate and address the situation. Remember to appreciate all the things that your partner is doing. No one wants to feel taken for granted. Learn to ask for what you want and need in a positive, productive way, rather than through complaining, accusing, or fighting. End the conversation with what you see as the solution.

"girl" talk

LET'S HEAR FROM OUR BOY JIM

We wanted to include Jim in this book because as someone raised by two working parents and now a working dad himself, he offers a unique point of view on these issues. From what we can see, he is also someone who has his priorities straight (giving enough to work to have significant responsibilities while spending quality time with a son who adores him).

So you were a latchkey kid. We don't hear that phrase used that often anymore.
When I was older, in fifth grade, I became a latchkey kid. We had some babysitters for nights my parents might be away, but we always came home from school ourselves, and it was not unusual for us to be alone in the afternoon.

What was the good, bad, and ugly about being a latchkey kid?
It was a real mixed bag that I think led to us being very independent. We had to be responsible for our afternoon activities, schoolwork, taking care of the house, feeding the cat, making sure our parents knew where we were, not fighting too much with my brother. That was all good for us in the long run. It was *not* easy re-

sisting my dad's stash of cookies, but we tried. The bad? What else? I loved my mommy and wished she was home. You fall and get hurt, you are alone. But you know what? It made us appreciate them more.

Did your parents miss a lot of your events, games, and other school activities?
Sure, on weekdays, especially my dad. But they always tried (and usually did make) evening games and weekends for sure.

How do you do things differently than your parents?
I play with my kid more for sure, especially sports. I think the value of play at a young age cannot be overstated. I avoid too strict a curriculum; I want my kid to have fun! I try to do what he wants to do at least a few days a week, not what I want.

What should working moms do to make their children feel loved and taken care of even if they miss activities because they are working?
Just take an interest in the activities and engage them. Make your children talk about it and never break a promise. I see how heart-broken my kid is at age five when I promise to be there and can't make it. I think the mom and all parents should try to find time to be at one game, one event a season, and not be afraid to tell the boss that's what you are doing.

How do you prioritize work and parenting?
It is so hard, right? Basically, I work my tail off at work, do a little personal work, and draw lines. I know the idea is 24/7, but I log off when I'm at home. I turn off my phone, IM, and 'Berry because I know I need to. My parents lived in a nine–five world and there is something to be said for that. I think we have become slaves to work and really many of us don't have to be, we just think we do. Home is for family first, and you need to draw those lines for your children.

traps we fall into

All of us reading, contributing, and writing this book have something in common. We are ambitious, perfection-seeking women who want to stand out at everything we attempt. We're not saying we want to have it all. We're saying we want, more than want, we *expect* to excel at everything we do. We've done well in school and in our careers. Now we're having babies, so we're going to be great mothers. And great partners to our significant others, too. The sad fact is we just can't do it all well all the time. Sometimes something has to give—work, motherhood, marriage—choose one. And that's what this chapter is all about—successfully navigating the negative traps to help us make better choices. Choices that will help us be better wives, mothers, and career girls. None of this is easy, and much of it is downright unpleasant. But forewarned is forearmed—and so we go ably forward and we offer some ways to avoid the five most common traps we fall into.

trap #1: vilifying and/or romanticizing stay-at-home moms

Sadly, there remains a lot of tension between stay-at-home moms and stay-working moms. For the working moms, the ones at home appear to be quickly going brain dead, more interested in *The Back-yardigans* than Baghdad. For the moms at home, the ones heading into offices each morning seem selfish and shallow, more interested in their careers and mani/pedis than their children.

Sigh.

Why the passing of all this judgment? Could it be because none of us are 100 percent satisfied with our decision and secretly wonder if we got it wrong? Could it be because some of us wish we could have a little more choice in the matter—we work because we need the money, and many of us stay home because it's cheaper than child care?

Does jealousy contribute to the great divide? The stay-at-home mom longs for what she thinks is a more stimulating environment while the working mom longs for more quality time with her children? There is also a whole lot of projecting going on. We had one interviewee tell us that she has been "envious of stay-at-home moms because they seem to build in more socialization time for themselves and their children, have time for exercising and hobbies and have done a good job of building support systems and staying connected."

When we first read this answer we immediately thought of a handful of women who have, in fact, figured out how to have it all while on the clock at home, but then we remembered the other 95 percent who were just as confused about the choice to opt out. You see, there is no one-size-fits-all solution to getting what you want out of life while being a great parent, spouse, friend, daughter, colleague, employer, and employee.

Whatever the reasons for the rift that keeps on growing, we simply don't appreciate how difficult it is for all of us. We all know how hard it is to be at home with children. They take an enormous amount of energy, time, and attention. It's exhausting and depleting in a way that work just isn't. On the other hand, working while parenting is as challenging but in a different way. When you work and parent you are managing two different lives, each with relationships and responsibilities. You can't let anyone down because the stakes are so high.

What we have in common is this: Both of our jobs (don't kid yourself that running a household and parenting full-time is anything but a job) require us to put others first. So rather than beat each other up about what we're not and what we should be, let's support one another. It may make all of our lives a little easier because the truth is we're actually not that different. It's time we appreciated that and united.

Relationships with other parents are important, whether they work or stay at home. Other mothers could have the answers you are looking for when it comes to how to get your child to sleep before midnight, or how to get him to eat carrots. Why do you want to rule out a huge chunk of the population as a potential resource or friend just because she made a different personal choice than you? Not only can you meet lifelong friends on the playground, but one working mom we spoke to told us that she relies on stay-at-home moms because they "are so helpful with school and practice drop-offs or pick-ups if you can't get off of work in time." Although, don't take too much advantage, this is exactly the kind of scenario that leads to resentment. Lorraine Nellis tells us that "Maintaining friendships with other parents is a great way to know what your kids are doing at all times."

Like politics and religion, working moms versus stay-at-home moms is a topic often best left out of discussion at a dinner party. Unfortunately, each side has clung to their distinct and divergent view, leaving little room for any gray area or respectful discourse. We'd like to try and change that; we'd like all moms to start focusing on our similarities and not our differences. Maybe there won't ever be a truce (though we can hope), but can there be a little more understanding? Civility and consideration can go a long way in this world. There is no one way to parent a child. In other words—in case we haven't driven the point home yet—all stay-at-home moms are not the same and all working mothers are not the same. The choices do not define the woman and they shouldn't pigeonhole others' opinions of them. But it often does and the debate gets heated and women end up skewering one another instead of supporting one another. In the end, does it make you feel more confident as a mother, better about your working situation, superior to the woman who has the different life?

No. So what's the point?

For a little light on the situation, we go to Oprah. On her show, women took part in a heated and often nasty debate about the choices they and those around them had made. But the results of an Oprah.com poll, in which more than fifteen thousand women (working mothers and stay-at-home mothers) responded, show the divide might not be as great as we think.

from stay-at-home moms:

Do stay-at-home moms get the respect they deserve?
    5 percent—Yes
    85 percent—No

Do you wish you worked?
    36 percent—Yes
    64 percent—No

Overall, are you satisfied with the job you are doing as a parent?

80 percent—Yes

20 percent—No

Would you describe your children as happy?

97 percent—Yes

3 percent—No

Is it possible to give 100 percent to motherhood and a career?

71 percent—Yes

29 percent—No

from working moms:

Do stay-at-home moms get the respect they deserve?

17 percent—Yes

83 percent—No

Would you quit to stay home if you could?

66 percent—Yes

34 percent—No

Overall, are you satisfied with the job you are doing as a parent?

71 percent—Yes

29 percent—No

Would you describe your children as happy?

93 percent—Yes

7 percent—No

Is it possible to give 100 percent to motherhood and a career?

61 percent—Yes

39 percent—No

the word

IT'S MORE THAN BAKE SALES AND CARPOOLING

Stay-at-home moms work hard, too. They may not be career girls like us, but many of them contribute to their communities in ways that we could only imagine and that benefit all of us. Their stories are as inspiring as those of women juggling work and family. Jennifer Heth should be the poster girl for a mother who has this job.

Service and volunteerism have been an intrinsic part of Jen's life since she was a young girl. She volunteered during high school and college and, armed with a journalism degree, was accepted into the Peace Corps after college. She was stationed in the Dominican Republic and responsible for establishing a Parent Teacher Association and convincing the community to become involved with the local school and their children's education. She's also a girl who operates best with a full plate and thrives on being busy.

After the Peace Corps, Jen moved home to Colorado and got married. She and her husband moved to a nice neighborhood in downtown Denver and decided to start a family. Jen was working as the marketing director of the nonprofit Denver Children's Museum. In that job, Jen worked twelve-hour days and many nights and weekends. She knew that she wouldn't be able to create the kind of family she wanted without making a change.

When she was pregnant with Emma, she decided not to return to her job. She gave her employer ample notice and even helped find and train her replacement. As a manager she had more than a few bad experiences with women who went out on maternity leave, planning to come back, only to tell her two weeks before they were expected back that they weren't returning.

She planned to stay home with Emma for six to twelve months and then start looking for a new job. Shortly after Emma was born, Jen's mother was diagnosed with terminal cancer. Jen spent the next year raising her daughter and taking care of her ailing mother. Eighteen months after Emma was born, Jen's mother died.

"I needed the time with Emma, and I needed to grieve for my mother," Jen said when recalling this time. "My mother and I were very close. I think after she died, it reinforced the mother-daughter bond I was creating with Emma."

Six months later, Jen landed a job where she could work from home. As the marketing manager for a nonprofit, Denver Telecomm, she organized meetings, members, and conferences. It worked out great until Charlie was born. While Emma had been a great sleeper, Charlie never slept. He didn't nap, he never wanted to be put down, and he constantly needed attention. Jen put Emma in preschool three days a week, quit her job, and poured herself into her kids.

Sending her kids to public school was a priority for Jen and her husband. As their local school district was populated with affluent families, many of them chose to send their children to private school. To increase enrollment, the local school became a magnet school for the deaf and hard-of-hearing as well as offering a traditional curriculum and a program for the gifted. Many of the students were bused in from other parts of the city. It led to an interesting and diverse student population but little parental involvement in the school.

A combination of Jen's professional training and her personal convictions led her to become very active in the school almost immediately after Emma enrolled. She spent Emma's kindergarten year volunteering and assessing what was needed. When Emma started first grade, she had a plan to present to the principal. Her year of observation and research led her to a couple of conclusions: The school needed a PTA and an enrichment program that wasn't available just to the gifted and talented, but one that was available to all of the student body.

Jen got to work. She became the president of the PTA and began recruiting parents and running fund-raising activities. She also began to formulate the enrichment program. Throughout this her goal was to create programs and systems that other parents could be trained for and take over. When the PTA was up and running, she tackled the enrichment program, which presented a number of unique challenges.

The goals for the program were to include all of the students from kindergarten to fifth grade; to mix them up so they could meet other children in the school of other ages and backgrounds; and to offer a wide range of activities that the students could choose for themselves. To do this required energy, principal buy-in, and funding.

Jen wrote and won a grant from the city of Denver, got the PTA to match it (because her fund-raising efforts had been so successful, there was a surplus of money), and set about to create the programs. During this, we should mention that she was a full-time mother of two kids and handled all of the responsibilities at home while also carving out time for herself. Her husband's job required a lot of travel and his schedule was very unpredictable. We should also remind our readers that she wasn't being paid to do any of this.

The program was finally ready. Armed with $4,500 and a cadre of volunteer instructors from the community whom she had recruited, she launched the first session of the enrichment program, with twenty-five classes offered every Friday afternoon in four-week sessions. The classes were all taught by professionals in the community, were available to 350 students, and included cooking, yoga, architecture, martial arts, cultural studies, animal care, fire-fighting, and various sports. They ran three sessions throughout the year.

The program was so successful that the agency that awarded Jen the original grant, Community Resources, has adopted it and is marketing it to other school districts in Colorado. They also did a very smart thing. They offered Jen a part-time job running one of their other programs. She is now working part-time for Community Resources, raising her family, running the enrichment program for the school that Charlie now attends (this will be her last year, as she's got a new team almost trained and ready to go), and is setting her sights on the middle school.

We think she should run for office. Seriously.

trap #2: hiding out at work

Work is our safe place. We can control it and most days have a really good time when we are there. We use our brains to solve problems, work under deadline pressure, and get paid for what we do. We believe we're good mothers because we work and we'll admit it: Many days we'd rather be at work than at home, changing diapers, running after toddlers, or arguing with our partners about who's going to get up in the middle of the night.

When we searched "hiding at work" on www.workitmom.com, one of our favorite working-mom blog sites (check out the sidebar later in this chapter for more), we found this one from Diane, who works at home: "I shut myself in the bedroom to get a project finished. Well, I want to share my little secret: I'm done, but I'm hiding in here just enjoying the relative silence, the pit-pat of rain on the roof, and surfing the Web. Every now and then a horde of dogs, cats, and a toddler can be heard clamoring outside the door wanting in. Hee hee. I wonder how long I can stay in here . . . ??"

Diane's hiding is perfectly harmless. It's when hiding evolves to avoiding that problems can occur. Kim knows this all too well. As a business owner and primary earner for her family, she could always rationalize the extra hours at night in the office or the time on the weekend. Her son wasn't suffering. He was with his father or grandmothers. Her marriage, however, was a different story.

Here are some ways to stop hiding:
- Ruth Klein in her book *"Time Management Secrets for Working Women: Getting Organized to Get the Most out of Each Day"* (Sourcebooks, Inc, 2005) recommends "The Three-Ds Filing System," which we like. The Ds stand for "Do it this morning," "Do it this afternoon," and "Do it now." We can apply it easily to our e-mail in-box, which has become our de facto

to-do list. When you get to work, open your e-mail and organize the Three Ds. Be realistic about what you can get done in
one day and don't forget to factor in time-sucking meetings
and conference calls. When you've gotten all of those things
done, go home to your family (or run to the gym—as we keep
reminding you, one of the secrets to happy working motherhood is for your life to include more than just work and mothering).

- Schedule the nights you need to work late in advance. If your
  child or spouse knows that one night a week you need to work
  late or attend evening work functions, then you are no longer
  hiding. You've set the expectation for your schedule. Now stick
  to it. Nothing upsets children (and spouses for that matter)
  more than constantly changing the schedule.

- Honor your commitments. If you've promised your family you
  will be home for dinner, go home and eat—even if you have
  heaps of work to do. You can always work remotely after the
  kids go to bed or get up early the next morning.

- Make sure you include a little down time in your day, even if
  it's just to read a magazine, listen to the radio, or sit quietly on
  your commute. A little break from work and mothering and the
  needs of others may be all the recharge you require.

trap #3: buckling under the weight of guilt

Oh, the mother guilt. Blogs, Web sites, and psychologists' couches
are filled with mothers describing their daily feelings of guilt. Every
single working mom we interviewed for this book mentioned the
guilt they feel about any number of aspects of their lives. And the
guilt begins before your baby is even born. Linda Barnes Gray, a college librarian from Tyler, Texas, and mother of two, tells us: "After

reading a number of books, I thought about going without any drugs to deliver my first and then my husband said people no longer bite a bullet for surgery, why should I go without pain medication? He made sense, but so many women (and so many books!) are so adamant about the effects of medication on the baby. In the end, my baby was in distress and I had to have a C-section, so all my guilt was for nothing. And then I picked up a book that had a chapter on breast-feeding with the following chapter about bottle feeding, which was laden with guilt trips about not breast-feeding. It made me pretty angry, since breast-feeding is not for everyone. I believe if it is not good for mom, it is not good for baby, since they can feel our stress."

All mothers feel guilt occasionally, but ample evidence suggests that working moms face an inordinate amount of guilt, especially from outside sources and most heart wrenchingly, when it comes from children themselves in the form of that dreaded question, "Mommy, why do you have to go to work?" Mother guilt will always exist whether we put it on ourselves or not. Our goal isn't to eradicate it but to manage it better. Based on the recommendations of the experts, our interviews, and personal experience, we've created a "Five-Step Program for Managing Mother Guilt."

1.   Assess if the guilt is deserved. Before you make a ruling, remember, by definition, guilt is an emotional experience that occurs when a person realizes or believes—whether justified or not—that she has violated a moral standard. A moral standard is a pretty strong litmus test, but if you can't be objective, ask your partner or working-mother friend to make the ruling. Most mother guilt is unwarranted. Chrisi Colabella expressed how many of us feel: "After my daughter Kali was born, I felt very guilty all of the time. I felt like I wasn't being a good mother, but I also felt like I wasn't working as hard as I

should." For the record, Chrisi changed her entire work schedule to spend more time with her daughter, hired extra people to cover the missing time at work, and reduced her pay to offset the additional head count. Kim feels guilty that she can't be the room mother for her son's class, even though she knows she not only would hate it, but would be terrible in the role. Caitlin gets the "guilts" when she spends one-on-one time with her daughter—even though it means that her son is spending the equivalent time with his father. If the guilt is unwarranted, then let it go. Just like that. If the guilt is warranted, make amends. A heartfelt apology is an easy place to start.

2. Assess your priorities, create your boundaries, and stick to them. If you've set up a four-day workweek to spend more time with your child, then don't work on your child's time. And vice versa. If you are telecommuting, don't play with your child on work time. If it's important that you take your child to the doctor, then take her. Make up the time you missed from work on your own time. Breaking promises and commitments leads to guilt, so stick to your word.

3. If the guilt is coming from an external source, then stop it as quickly as possible. Don't apologize (remember, you didn't do anything wrong). Explain why the guilt trip that is being laid on you is inappropriate and move on. If you are dealing with habitual guilters (such as Kim's grandmother, who has done post-doctorate work in guilt-tripping), then minimize your contact with them.

4. Just say no. Much of our guilt stems from the feeling of letting others down. If we don't make the commitments in the first place, we can't let anyone down, and we don't feel guilty.

5. Forgive yourself. You will make mistakes. You will be overextended, overscheduled, and overwhelmed. It's okay. We've all

been there. Go back to step one. Make amends and try to learn from your error.

trap #4: not appreciating ourselves

After interviewing the hundreds of women for all of our books, we realized that we all suffer from the same thing: We don't appreciate ourselves. We discount and downplay how much we accomplish in a day and minimize how hard it really is. We can all find someone who is doing more or juggling more than we are. It doesn't mean we're not juggling a lot. And all of a sudden before you know it, you are piling more and more on your plate and eventually something gives, and for many of the women we've talked to, it's their health. Stress-related illnesses are real and prevalent. Irritable bowel syndrome, temporomandibular joint disorder, migraine, take your pick.

Laurice, a mother of four boys (three of whom are triplets) and owner of a cleaning business, has been suffering from debilitating migraines for the past year and doctors can't find a cause. None of the migraine medications are working. She describes her situation: "The doctor did mention that it would certainly help to eliminate as much stress as possible, avoid caffeine, and get a good night's sleep. How interesting . . . I get woken many nights, I drink Diet Coke and tea daily, and I've spent almost every waking moment this entire summer with three seven-year olds and a five-year old while running a business. I think a weekly root canal may be less stressful!"

We couldn't agree more, but she continues: "I'm being funny and my husband is fantastic! My business does not take that much of my time and the kids are pretty good, and my husband is very hands-on. I have to start taking better care of myself. I need to drink more water, lay off the caffeine, etc. Things I know to do, I just don't always actually do."

Laurice is not unusual. Most of the women we talk to minimize the challenges they handle on a daily basis and take too much blame for what doesn't go right. Would Laurice's headaches go away if she drank more water and slept more? Maybe. But is that really the point? Isn't the point that she's managing a ton every day, which she discounts, and then when something suffers (her health), she blames herself because really it's no big deal to take care of a business, four kids, and a house all on your own because she has a supportive husband.

In 2000, Naomi G. Swanson published an article in the *Journal of the American Women's Medical Association* stating that "high-strain jobs have been linked with psychological distress, pain, and reduced physical functioning among nurses; increased sickness absenteeism and depressive symptoms among female workers in a wide variety of occupations; significant increases in blood pressure among more highly educated female white-collar workers; an increased risk of myocardial infarction; and more than twice the risk for short (24 days or less) menstrual cycles."

But the answer isn't to stop work. The article also showed that "overall, employment has many benefits for women, including increased financial resources, a sense of achievement, and reduced social isolation, all of which can benefit health. Additionally, some research has indicated that women who occupy multiple roles (mother, worker, spouse) experience better mental and physical health than women who occupy few roles, perhaps because with multiple roles, the stresses of one role may be offset by the rewards of another."

The kicker apparently, though, is when one of the role's negatives offsets the other's positives. For example, if you lose your child care due to a sick child, more often than not mothers leave work, therefore increasing stress. It's more of what we know—this job is really hard and when it gets off track it can make us sick. Swanson's article offers recommendations for how organizations can reduce stress for working mothers that include "expanding promotion and career ladders, introducing such family support programs as flexible schedules and dependent care programs and introducing clear, accessible, and enforced policies against sex discrimination and sexual harassment."

We would add that working mothers can reduce their own stress by asking for more help—especially when their health is being affected.

trap #5: seeking perfection

Oh, for overachieving women, good is just *not* good enough. We need to be perfect—at work, at home, in bed with our partners. When we asked working moms if they thought they were good mothers, they all answered that they "could be better if . . ." We know most of these women whom we polled. And they are great mothers. Why aren't they satisfied? Nicki's story will shed a little light on the topic.

girl talk

NICKI'S RELENTLESS, EXHAUSTING, AND WHOLLY UNNECESSARY PURSUIT OF PERFECTION

Nicki Dugan is the senior director of corporate communications at Yahoo! Unlike most of us, Nicki Dugan started worrying about the age-old balancing act of being a good mother with a dynamic career when she was seventeen years old. She even spoke to her high-school guidance counselor about it. She couldn't see a way to do everything well. In her recollection, she had the perfect mother—stay-at-home and always available to her—just the kind of mother Nicki wanted to be herself someday. And yet she also wanted a career.

Unable to reconcile this conundrum, she chased her work ambitions full-throttle. She started working at a magazine in New York City and, like all perfectionists, poured everything she had into it. Twelve-hour days were the norm—she was often the first one in and the last one to leave, and she got promoted quickly. At twenty-five, she married her college sweetheart and followed him to Hawaii, where he was stationed in the marine corps. She took a job in public relations and continued to excel. She was driven by a fear of mediocrity and gave 100 percent in everything she took on.

Having a family was always in the plan for her and her husband, but they kept putting it off—in part because of Nicki's "can't do it all" fear. She and her husband eventually moved to San Francisco and became part of the dot-com revolution. She landed a job at Yahoo!, where she remains. But work was only one part of Nicki's life. She was a devoted wife, avid gardener, creative cook, jewelry maker, and social organizer. She also became obsessed with running marathons.

At thirty-four and after nine years of marriage she opted for motherhood. In fact, she found out later that she ran her tenth marathon three weeks' pregnant. And, as we learned from Nicki, being a perfect career girl, wife, friend, and mother was harder than she had ever imagined at seventeen. She shares her hard-learned lessons with the rest of us.

How did your work life change after you had Max [Nicki's first child]?
I had been at Yahoo! for two years by the time I got pregnant, working sixty-hour weeks right up until my due date. When I came back after maternity leave, I felt like I had lost in musical chairs, but

I didn't do anything to reclaim my seat. For the first time in my life, I voluntarily took a backseat in my job. I was afraid of putting my neck out the way I had always done before because I just didn't think I would be able to pull it off. I stopped going for high-profile projects because I knew I had to be home to relieve the nanny. I skulked out at 5:00 p.m. knowing that the others would be there long into the night, as I always had. It really set me back.

But we thought Yahoo! was a family-friendly place?
The irony is that it actually is family friendly—I mean as family friendly as a Web company can be. But there weren't many Yahoo! mothers at the time. And I put the pressure, the unrealistic expectations, and the paranoia squarely on myself. My colleagues later told me that, as I snuck home at night, they thought, "Hey, she's a good mother." Meanwhile, I beat myself up as "one of those slackers."

I tried to compartmentalize my life unnecessarily. I rarely spoke about Max in the office, not wanting to draw attention to my new "career handicap," and I was constantly feeling both guilty about my parenting and frustrated that my career had stalled. There were days when I'd cry in the mother's room, full of guilt about having to take time out to pump as my peers raced around. But when I walked in and found our very accomplished CFO's gear in there one day (she was on her third kid), it gave me new perspective on these conflicting emotions. It helped me stop feeling like a horrible mother and I stopped beating myself up about work, but it didn't really improve until after my second son was born.

We're listening to your story and asking ourselves where was your husband in all of this? Why did you have to get home to relieve the nanny? Why did you have to take a backseat at work? Why weren't you making him more responsible for coparenting?
When Max was born, my husband was in a consulting position that required him to be out of town Monday through Friday, so the nanny (and she was extraordinary) and I did everything. He would return home on Friday night, full of questions about how to take care of his own son. I resented him but felt like caring for Max was

more my responsibility because I was the mother. "I am the one who can breast-feed and I am the one who can get it done, so I will." Aside from changing diapers, there were so few things I ever really asked him to do. Something had to give, so my husband hired a cleaning lady. Instead of thinking it was a great thing, all I could think was that if I didn't do it myself, I was a failure.

How did you get back in the groove?
I think what changed all of that for me was getting some really tough feedback in a review. The first bad review I had ever had. I think some of it was unfair, but she basically made me realize I was putting this baggage on myself, and because of this baggage I wasn't contributing anymore and something had to change. I could have quit then, but I didn't want to. As hard as it was to hear, my boss was right. I had changed. I had to prove to myself that my old self was there—I just needed to find her again.

In addition to the bad review, she also gave me an opportunity to birth a big project for the company. It was an awesome challenge and mine to own from start to finish. I am really glad that I stuck it out because through it all I found a way to ask for more help at home so I could get the project done. I also finally regained my confidence.

Any words of advice?
My biggest regret in some ways was that I didn't have the confidence to jump back into work with both feet after Max was born. It would have made those years so much easier. I let "working mother" become the oxymoron I'd always feared it would be. I expected far too much of myself and created a self-fulfilling prophecy that left me living in constant turmoil. As I pureed homemade organic baby food at midnight (after all, I had to be perfect), I felt the creeping anxiety of all the work I should be doing instead. And vice versa.

Now I try to apply the deathbed test as I pick my battles. Isn't this Halloween parade more important in the long run than going to the office? Isn't this work project better for our family than chaperoning that field trip? I've finally realized that the world won't stop if I take a time-out from either work or family. The theme of my life has been a constant pursuit of perfection, and the fact that I couldn't be near the same person I was before I had my children was hard to accept. But what I realized is that good enough sometimes just has to be good enough. And I finally give myself credit for all the things I accomplish in a day. But it's a process getting to a new place. I still don't delegate enough to my husband and I occasionally beat myself up when I think I could've done a better job. And I still haven't made it to surf camp. But it's on my list—I promise.

keeping your career alive

Becoming a mother offers a unique opportunity to take a step back and decide what you want from your job. You could simply be in it for the money or you could realize, as our friend Leigh Ann did during her maternity leave, your career is an essential part of your identity. The key is to have a work situation that supports and offers you what you need from a job as a working mom: money, security, inspiration, motivation, and flexibility. Once you have taken a moment to look in the mirror at the new professional you, taken stock of the time and energy now required of you at home, and reviewed your new financial landscape, you can begin your list of job requirements. These are the qualities—pay, benefits, hours, opportunities—that will help you plan your next steps, whether that is asking for a change in your schedule or looking for a new career altogether. Whichever way you want to go, this chapter will help you figure out if you need to reconfigure your current job or look for something new altogether, where to start, and whom to turn to for help.

your crystal ball

If you could look into the crystal ball and see the future, would you be surprised with what you see? If you've set clear goals for yourself, the answer should be no. Of course, unexpected things always come up (see Girl Talk: Dr. Nicole Lamborne), but your life (and especially your work life) shouldn't be a total surprise.

If you can't predict the future, it's probably because, like us, you've been trying to do so much for so long and at such a fast speed that you have lost sight of what you want. If anything, working on this book has really taught us the power of choice. Most of the working moms who shared their stories with us, even though they struggle and have made mistakes, are optimistic about the future and the potential their careers still hold.

It's important to review your goals now so the crystal ball won't reveal too many surprises.

Girl's Guide tips for effective goal-setting

1. You gotta want it. When setting goals for yourself and your family, make sure you focus on things that you really want and not just what "you're supposed" to want. Do you really want to be the boss in five years or is being the right hand to the boss a better role for you? If you don't really want it, it won't happen. Sometimes, though, you don't find out until you give it a chance. Ever since we published our first book, people have been telling us we should get a television show. Producers, agents, friends, you name it, they've told us we need a reality show. Well, after five years of not making any progress (and it's the only thing we've ever set our minds to that hasn't hap-

pened), we realized we didn't really want to star in a television show. Caitlin wants to produce one, so she is working to make that happen instead, and we have no doubt that it will happen.

2. One goal can't get in the way of another—which is actually the trap that many working women fall into. Our prime working years coincide with our prime baby-making years and you need to plan around it. Physically, mentally, and emotionally, you just can't give that much energy to your career and baby. Take a longer view, know that you'll be a little slower when the kids are young, but have ample opportunity to make up the time.

3. Be positive when setting goals. We have fallen into this trap for years. Our thinking focused on what we didn't want to do— take on a new client or hire a new person, for example—versus what we did want, which was to grow both businesses slowly and steadily so that we could work less.

4. Write your goals down on paper and be as specific as possible. "I want a promotion and raise" is not an effective goal statement. You need to spell out the terms: "I want to be the marketing director running a department of twenty and making $150,000 in three years."

5. Aim high. You haven't come this far in your career and life to start thinking small now. You are a working mother, you're already a superstar.

the word

HOW TO SUCCEED IN BUSINESS WHEN I SHOULD BE OUT FREEZING MY EGGS

Elissa Ellis Sangster is the executive director for the Forté Foundation, an organization dedicated to inspiring women business leaders. Prior to her position with Forté, Elissa served as the assistant dean and director of the M.B.A. program at the McCombs School of Business at the University of Texas at Austin and saw firsthand the issues affecting women's abilities to seek, prepare for, and attain business leadership positions.

Elissa has an M.B.A. herself and believes that M.B.A.s are important for women because to really succeed in business you need to be bold and confident when you walk through the doors of big business (or a big bank when you need money for your start-up business!). According to Elissa, "An M.B.A. is extremely empowering. It provides a set of skills and a way of thinking that is really valued in the marketplace. Its broad curriculum teaches you to be a critical thinker, a problem-solver and entrepreneurial in all things. And most importantly, you will create a network for life, of friends and colleagues who you can count on and connect with for your entire careers. It's also a lot of fun."

The median age for students in an M.B.A. program is twenty-eight and your prime career years begin the second you graduate—once again coinciding with your prime family years. This fact is not lost on the women in the programs. Most women M.B.A.s want to know when they should plan to have their kids. Elissa shared: "At one conference, an attendee asked a panelist if she should consider freezing her eggs since she was already thirty-five. The panelist told her she should have frozen her eggs at twenty-seven. The women in the room looked as if they were going to get up en masse to run out and get their eggs frozen."

Elissa's recently gotten married for the first time and at forty is trying to create a family of her own. Her work with the Forté Foundation has given her the opportunity to travel all over the country meeting businesswomen. Elissa offers some thoughts about successful women business leaders:

- Find the right partner. Don't marry somebody until you have conversations about how you want your life to look after having babies. Don't accept a partner who's not going to be supportive of your decision to keep working.
- Even with the most enlightened partners, the burden of responsibility lands on women. Be prepared for it.

- The hard part is changing the business culture that has made a focus on "face time" and being in the office. Gen X wants more flexibility, and as they move into senior leadership positions, the culture will change. Women are going to be a big part of this change. But it's going to take time.

girl talk

THERE'S NO SUCH THING AS A PART-TIME DOCTOR

Dr. Nicole Lamborne is the mother of three children and an obstetrician/gynecologist in a private practice and clinic in southern New Jersey. She is married to a pediatrician whom she met in her first year of medical school.

Nicole is an extraordinary woman, so it's no surprise to us that her working motherhood journey has been an extraordinary one as well. Nicole got pregnant in her third year of residency—quite by accident. Yes, you read that correctly, a third-year resident in obstetrics married to a third-year resident in pediatrics had an unplanned pregnancy. Nicole forgot to take her birth control pill one day and because of their crazy schedules she and her husband had sex only one time that month!

She never imagined she could be pregnant when she started feeling sick at work. No one in their right mind would get pregnant during their residency. The shifts are thirty-six-hours long. But since she was in training to be a doctor, she decided to treat herself as one of her patients and took a home pregnancy test (during her shift at work). She also had some light spotting, so to rule out a miscarriage she had a friend from her residency sneak with her into an examining room after their shifts ended to do an ultrasound. They saw a heartbeat. Nicole was indeed pregnant.

She did not have the kind of job where you call in sick to work. At her hospital, if you were sick, you came to work, strapped yourself to an I.V. for thirty minutes, and then got back on the job. She was in a competitive program too. The last thing she wanted anyone to know was that she was pregnant. She was able to keep her pregnancy a secret for five months, even though she frequently had to scrub out of a surgery and throw up.

At five months she went to her program director with a plan to complete her residency on time. She would work right through her pregnancy and take maternity leave instead of doing the four weeks of service work that she had planned to do in Bolivia. Even though Nicole and her husband had always planned on having a family, this was not the timing she envisioned, so she just worked through her pregnancy as if nothing was different. She ignored all the signs that she needed to take it easy (doctors do make the worst patients!) and went into preterm labor. After a serious talk with her chief resident, she agreed to take it easy. Her daughter was delivered healthy at full term. Nicole went back to work four weeks later, but it was much harder than she expected. She wanted to quit her residency and stay home with her daughter. After a lot of soul-searching and discussions with her husband, she decided to finish her residency, get her board certification, and then quit working to stay home with her baby. That didn't happen.

As of this writing, Nicole has three children—eight, five, and three—and is a practicing obstetrician and gynecologist. Ideally she would work less, but she shares with us the trade-offs she's made in search of solutions to create the life that she wants with her family and work. Her journey hasn't been easy, and it's not even complete, but we applaud and admire her effort. She inspires us because if she can make it work and maintain the hope of achieving her ultimate schedule and balance, then there is hope for us all.

We're shocked that you wanted to quit working to raise your children. You are a doctor—and have ostensibly worked toward that goal your entire life!

I know. It doesn't make that much sense. I never thought I could feel about a child the way I felt about Gabriella when she was born. When I was with her I was so incredibly happy, nothing else mattered. I was in a dilemma. I loved being with Gabriella and I had worked my entire life to be a doctor (not to mention the amount of debt that I had built up in the effort). If I didn't finish my residency and get board certified, then I was giving up ever becoming a doctor.

I often think that intense jobs attract intense people who just can't figure out how to do anything halfway. You want to throw yourself into it 100 percent. If I am a doctor, then I want to be the best doctor, and simultaneously I also want to be the best mother I can be. I just didn't know how to do it. So I organized my priorities and took all the perks that being a chief resident would offer and went back to work.

Chief residents can do things that third years couldn't. My attending physician liked me and I had been an exemplary resident up until that point. So I figured, if I had to leave to pick up Gabriella, I had to leave.

I was on call from 6 a.m. to 6 p.m. and Gabriella was in a home day care. We had my mom as a backup, so if Harry (Nicole's husband) or I got caught in surgery, then my mother would pick her up.

My other priority was breast-feeding. No other new mothers had ever been in the program, so there was no model to follow. I would tell people I was going to pump and nobody said a word. The hardest part was when I was stuck in surgery or an emergency C-section; then I would miss my window. But I had dedicated myself to it, so I stuck with it.

I looked at work the same way. I had dedicated myself to it and was now going to see it through to board certification. I went through the checklist: Pass the written test at the end of the residency, complete a big research project, find a part-time private practice job where I could get enough experience to sit for my oral boards, get board certified, and quit to stay home with Gabriella.

But you're still working?
I know. When I started looking for a job, I was clear that I didn't want to be a high-powered doctor who wanted to see a million patients. I wanted to have time to be with my family. My ideal was a part-time role, but no one would take someone on part-time be-

cause the cost of malpractice is so high. And in obstetrics you had to be willing to cover other doctors' shifts.

When you first come out of residency, you are a physician whose salary is paid either by a group health system or a private practice. I found a private physician who needed help and was willing to let me work less if I took less pay. I planned on joining his practice when my fourth year finished. During the time I was finishing school, he took on another partner so by the time I started, I had two bosses instead of one and the new partner demanded that I do equal work. It was a little less than twice what I was doing and they would pay me more. I agreed to come up to full-time with them; because I was the youngest in the group, I wanted to prove my worth and pull my weight and then go part-time.

So it sounds like this part-time doctor thing really isn't an option. It's funny, I just kept thinking, if I just do this one more thing, then I will get a part-time situation. That first year was really tough on me and Harry. His job was particularly demanding, with long hours and lots of weekends. We tried to coordinate our weekend schedules so that we wouldn't both be on call because we'd have to ship Gabriella off to her grandparents. That year we had to leave her with Harry's parents Christmas Day because we were both on call the day after Christmas.

It didn't feel right and we didn't want to continue long term but couldn't come up with any solutions yet. I was happy in my job at this point and I felt rewarded. One of my partners then got pregnant and offered me a bonus if I would cover her maternity leave. We needed the money (we both had so much school debt), and since I was building a practice, it seemed to make sense.

Harry, on the other hand, was miserable in his job and decided to go back to the hospital, where he had set hours. Set hours were great, but the ninety-minute drive to work each way that he took on wasn't. It was very stressful, and if our daughter was sick it was on me, and our practice just kept getting busier.

Right before my partner went out on maternity leave, I got pregnant with Michaela. I know you must think I am crazy with everything else that we were juggling, but Gabriella was almost two and I didn't want only one child and I didn't want them to be too spaced apart. I needed to do it now or it wasn't going to happen. I tell my patients all the time, there's no good time to have a baby.

I thought if I could just get a little more help, I could handle it, and it's almost time to take my oral boards and once I am board certified I can finally work part-time.

So how did it go with Michaela?
I felt physically very well with Michaela, ate well, and slept more, but I have a heart problem so I was being careful.

Did you just say you had a heart problem?
Oh sorry, yes. They found the hole in my heart during my pregnancy with Gabriella. There's nothing they can really do until you have a problem, like a stroke. Basically it would just make me tired, and I have a low heart rate because my heart is working much harder.

But I was feeling good and work was going well. The only challenge was that without the help of my extended family or Harry, I was going to have to make a change when Michaela was born.

I was offered a partnership in May and decided not to take it. I felt that for the health of our family, it made more sense to make a change and move closer to my job. My plan had always been to cut back, and if I signed on as full partner I would never cut back.

I called my mentor from medical school to help me figure out a job where I could balance my family life and my career. She called me back a day later and offered me a job working in her practice with a group of five.

I was moving toward a better life, more regular hours, less stress, more doctors, and when I was covering labor and delivery, I didn't have to do patient hours in the office too, so that would leave me more energy. With OB work, it's not just the hours that you put in, it's the intensity of them.

In January 2004, just after Michaela turned one, I passed my oral boards and started my new job. The change was huge. We were closer to Harry's job, which required no evenings or weekends, and I had a much better schedule. Between those factors and being closer to my mom, I was feeling really good.

I didn't feel like I was done having children after Michaela and realized I wanted one more. And when we got married Harry always wanted three. When Michaela was eighteen months old I got pregnant with Nicholas.

Okay, what happened next?
It's a long story, but the short story is that I had a stroke and had to get my heart repaired. Nicholas's delivery was really difficult but he was fine, and after I recovered, I realized I was back to the way I felt with Gabriella. I didn't get the bonding time in the beginning and I was two months back at work, then I had a really difficult case where a woman had lost her baby. It emotionally destroyed me and I didn't want to be a doctor anymore.

Please tell us there's a happy ending.
Actually, there is. Although the opportunity for part-time work hasn't happened, I have found a great job with Our Lady of Lourdes health system. They offered me a job working at a clinic in Camden, N.J., with set hours. I resigned from my practice and accepted. A couple of my patients wanted to follow me, so Our Lady of Lourdes set me up with an office to see patients privately one day a week.

It started out as a small little extra thing that I did and it just grew and grew. After a month, we realized I needed to make it a real practice. It's been working so far. The clinic work really rejuvenated me. I always wanted to do service work, and with my small practice and the clinic, practicing medicine is making me happy again.

I still struggle with wanting to be a mom and be present more, but I haven't added evening or weekend hours. My plan is to build this private practice over three or four years and add other doctors. As the original member of the group, I will get a bigger draw. By the time it's all up and running, my school loans and the bulk of our mortgage will be paid off. I like delivering babies, but I am happiest with my children. With the new job, I've requested Gabriella's swim meets off and I've made a bunch of Michaela's soccer games, too.

I remind my kids, I am not the only parent who works or has a demanding job. I think Gabriella is starting to get it. She loves telling her friends that her mom delivers babies and her daddy takes care of them.

time for a change

It's pretty impossible for an obstetrician to work part-time or from home, but that's certainly not the case for most positions. The corporate world is changing dramatically right now. As we become a global workforce and communication technology continues to improve, the need to be in an office every day has diminished significantly in the last ten years. Many jobs still require face time to get ahead, but more often than not, management is interested in results, and if you can prove that you will be more productive in a less traditional working arrangement (part-time, flextime, job sharing, or telecommuting), then you should make a business case for it. You need to demonstrate that your productivity will actually increase if you have the flexibility to make your own schedule. Of course it's a scary change, but if your current situation isn't working then you really have nothing to lose by asking. Consider the following list.

It might be time to speak to your boss about a flexible schedule if you . . .
- Still enjoy the essence of your job
- Like your coworkers
- Have a supportive boss
- Feel that if you just had more flexible time then you could better juggle work and family responsibilities

- You can see yourself going back to full-time in a few years
- Don't see yourself as a stay-at-home mom
- Have the financial flexibility to work at a reduced salary

thinking about (and pitching) your options

In a perfect world we would have more flexibility in our schedules. There are a few options for you to explore if changing when and how you work is a priority for you. Before you consider any of the options we outline below, you need to do a little research. Work with your spouse to determine the ideal work schedule, how much you need to make to see if there is any wiggle room on the salary, and if you are thinking of spending any time working at home, do you have the space to set up a home office? Then, look at your job responsibilities to see if you could honestly make the case for telecommuting, job sharing, or compressing your schedule. For those who manage a big staff, it is unlikely you could sell your boss on you working from home, even for a day. But if you are part of a creative team somewhere and you already spend a chunk of the day working solo, then it might be easier to transition to telecommuting.

Look around the office to see if there is anyone else who has negotiated for a change in her schedule. It's always easier to get something if precedent has been set. If you want to go to part-time, be prepared for a significant pay cut. Asking for a part-time position could either be a huge relief for your boss because it saves money or it could be a huge burden for management if it means a pile of work that they would need to delegate. So know that asking for that radical shift in your job could go either way and you might end up looking elsewhere for the job solution.

If you have done your research both at home and at work, then go to your boss with a fully thought-out and detailed proposal. Be ready to make the case for how you are going to get your job done as efficiently as you do now. Illustrate how this would not make more work for your boss. That is what bosses care about at the end of the day. Demonstrate how you are set up to make a smooth transition by showing how you would manage delegating or working from home on existing projects. Before asking, employer and working mom Sarah Rubenstein advises, "Approach the issue as a proposal that you have given a lot of careful consideration to and come to the discussion with a few suggestions as to how you can make it work for both parties."

Going in confident, with your facts at your fingertips, will make it more difficult for your boss not to at least consider your request. You may want to proactively offer to try out the new situation before asking for any commitment from the company.

some of your flexible schedule options

FLEXTIME

This is an option that appeals to many of us. In fact, a 2000 study by the Radcliff Public Policy Center with Harris Interactive found that for women in their twenties, thirties, and forties, having a work schedule that allows them to spend more time with their families was *the* most important job characteristic. A flextime schedule could be a range of different arrangements, including working at the office for a partial day and working late at night to finish, compressing the workweek so you spend four long days but have that fifth day off.

JOB SHARING

Much rarer than flextime, job sharing is literally splitting your job with another employee. We know a few people who have done this, and its success is often contingent upon excellent communication between the coworkers. If you decide to share your job then you are essentially going down to part-time, so you will be taking a pay cut and your benefits may be impacted.

PART-TIME

Part-time employees work fewer hours or fewer days than full-time employees. They might be working three full days a week or five half days. They also might work only during certain parts of the year or have heavier schedules only during high seasons. Your salary as a part-time employee is reduced and it is more difficult to hold on to your benefits, but if you can swing it, then balancing everything at home can be significantly easier.

TELECOMMUTING

Telecommuting is working from home for someone else. It can be pretty amazing if all parties are comfortable with it. According to the U.S. Census Bureau back in 2001, 15 percent of us worked from home at least once a week, a number that's going up, since in 2004 the Office of Personnel Management found that more than 23 million of us telecommute either part-time or full-time. We have an interview at the end of this chapter with a woman who worked this arrangement out with her company, so make sure you read it if this setup appeals to you. Also read Pros and Cons of Telecommuting later in this chapter.

If you decide to pursue changing your work schedule with your current employer, then please go into the negotiation prepared. Timing is also essential, so make the "ask" when your standing at the company is at a peak. You are in a better position to get what you want when you can confidently demonstrate your experience and contribution to your boss. Being a great employee with a proven track record and knowing that you are an asset to the company make any request more likely to be granted.

FLEXTIME FACTS

According to the Sloan Work and Family Research Institute:

- Employees have fewer mental health problems when they have a flexible schedule.
- In 2002, 32 percent of workers with access to flexible work schedules reported no conflict between job and family life.
- In 2002, 34 percent of flexible workers had very little work negativity spill over into their homes.
- The National Study of the Changing Workforce survey in 2002 found that 73 percent of employees with flexible schedules reported a high likelihood they would stick with their current job for at least another year.
- Sixty-eight percent of companies allow employees to change starting or ending times.

the word

DOLLARS AND CENTS

We asked personal finance expert Galia Gichon (www.downto earthfinance.com) to share her top five financial steps to prepare for going to part-time.

1. Women don't take into account their time off. It isn't uncommon to take a break from the work world or go part-time, but if you do, be sure to invest in yourself. Continue to network in your industry, take consulting projects, keep up on business reading, and attend industry conferences. When you are ready to go back to work full-time or have more time to work, you will find that the time you had invested in yourself pays off.

2. Once you decide to go part-time, create a separate savings account just for the possibility of staying at home or increased expenses. If it is separate from your other savings, it will have more meaning. Also, make your savings automatic to an online savings account (i.e., ING Direct) and you will end up saving more—I see it over and over.

3. Because you are part-time, chances are you are not getting any benefits. At a minimum, create a Spousal IRA for yourself. You can contribute only up to $5,000 a year (in 2008), but it allows you to continue contributing to your retirement savings. If you are earning a good bit of income, consider setting up a SEP IRA. You can save money on taxes and put away a substantial amount into a tax-deferred account.

4. Focus on the big-money picture of how much you should be saving. Sure you know how much you need to pay your mortgage or rent, but do you know how much to save annually for your child's college education or to retire successfully? Schedule an appointment with a fee-only independent financial planner or take advantage of online financial calculators at kiplinger.com or money.com. Whether you save those calculations or not, it takes the guesswork out of the equation.

5. Bring positive money habits into your life on a weekly basis. See if any of your friends have great money behaviors that you want to learn and start practicing yourself. Start weekly coffee sessions to motivate each other to provide mutual support (i.e., a savings contest). Read a personal finance blog of someone who is trying to change their financial habits or bookmark a site that will help you focus on your money more regularly, such as geezo.com, a social networking site for your money, and wesave.com, similar to quicken.com or mint.com.

pros and cons of telecommuting

Working from home sounds ideal, doesn't it? You get the salary and benefits while having the freedom to work in your pajamas. Just like with every work situation, there are pros and cons to moving the office into your home.

The upsides of telecommuting
- There is more flexibility during the day to work when you work best.
- More work gets done without the endless interruptions, meetings, and socializing that goes on in most offices.
- You are free to create an office environment that inspires you.
- It's nice to be home near your children, and you can take advantage of that by having lunch or a snack with them during the day.
- No commuting time.
- You can have a freelance lifestyle without the financial concerns.

The downsides of telecommuting
- Your freedom is somewhat of an illusion.
- If you get a new boss or the company restructures, you could be back in the office within days because not everyone is okay with it.
- It is difficult to turn off the job when it's just a few doors (or feet) away.
- You may find yourself with a bigger workload as your ability to turn around work increases.
- With your children nearby, it can be hard to stay away and you may end up resenting having to close that office door.

a note from the authors about working from home

Both of us spent two years or so working out of our home offices. This was years ago and before we merged to launch YC Media (www.ycmedia.com). The office setups were similar in that we both had desks in the corners of our tiny apartments. Hey, they don't call them bedroom businesses for nothing. The first few months of working from home are often a dream—get up whenever you wake up, take a break when you feel like it, work out when you're in the mood, make yourself a delicious lunch, play with the kids, or let them interrupt you whenever they want a little mommy time. It's all pretty great as you get a taste of freedom during the work-week. Then you reach a fork in the road. You can either let your productivity continue to diminish, or you can start treating your workday like you did when you were steps away from your boss, not miles.

Obviously, we recommend taking control of your workday, because if you give in to the potential slothfulness you might lose your cushy gig. Start with the child care situation. To work efficiently and effectively, you absolutely must have some kind of child care because most jobs can't be squeezed in during nap and after bedtime. Set up a home office that offers private space and get a separate phone line. Get up early, take a shower, put on real clothes, and get to your desk when everyone else does. Commit to putting in a full day with a few benefits thrown in like lunch with your kids, a trip to the gym, or something else that lets you enjoy your situation.

We've now reviewed the flextime options and maybe you decided those wouldn't work for you or your employer has turned you down. Is it time to go? Read through the statements below and gauge the emotional ramifications and practical aspects of staying at your job.

It might be time to go if you . . .

- Dread going to work
- Can't give your best because of family obligations
- Have a boss who is far from supportive of working mothers
- See no working moms in senior positions
- No longer are passionate or even energized by the job
- Can't pay the new layer of bills with your salary and were turned down for a raise
- Feel like you can't be the kind of mom you want to be while working

beginning the job hunt

Now that you are a mom as well as a professional, your requirements for your next position may have changed, so before you start looking take stock of yourself, the situation, and your finances.

WHAT DO YOU HAVE TO GIVE?
Ask yourself how much you want and can give to your next job. Consider how your personal life has impacted your energy level, focus, biorhythms, and passion for your career and work with those facts. The new you just might be looking for something else these days, and it's important that you know what that is before you look for and take another gig.

HOW MUCH MONEY DO YOU NEED NOW?
Now that your situation has changed, you may also need a bigger salary than you originally thought. Before calling headhunters, do a household budget to see how much you need for monthly expenses. Add to that number how much you would like to add to savings or college plans in an ideal world. After looking at these household numbers you may feel really different about what your next job should pay.

YOUR SCHEDULE

Before starting to look for a new job, consider your schedule. Is your child care situation flexible or do you absolutely need to get home at a certain time? Could you save significant money on child care if you changed your work schedule? What is the ideal balance of work and home? Now, you may not find the perfect solution, but going into a job search with some clarity of your best situation may help you negotiate for something better.

BUILD THE NETWORK

There are so many ways to build your network these days. Many of us use LinkedIn to maintain and grow our virtual Rolodex. And although social networking sites are mostly used for socializing, the friends, former classmates, and acquaintances you may find there are worth contacting when you start looking for a job. There are professional organizations to join, former and current mentors to meet with. Don't think small when planning your next move. That holds especially true when it comes to tapping into your resources.

BE CLEAR ABOUT WHAT YOU WANT

To maximize any and all contacts and opportunities, have a clear vision of what you are looking for from your next job. As the founders of Girl's Guide (www.girlsguidetobusiness.com), we have gotten hundreds of e-mails from women asking for career advice or networking help. If the cold call e-mail includes a clear ask from us, such as someone is looking for an informational interview with someone in the public relations field or someone needs a few tips for how to start their own business, we can offer advice. So help your network help you by being direct and clear about what you want.

selling yourself in an interview

See above for our line about being clear with your network when you are looking for a job because the same holds true during an interview. Many new working moms (and those reentering the workforce) are unsure if and how to bring their personal situation into an interview. Reluctant to turn off a potential employer who might assume a working mom will be running out at 5 p.m. every night, most of us keep mum. Jamie Pennington, founder of Flexible Executives (www.flexibleexecutives.com), doesn't recommend this tactic. "Don't hesitate to say that you are the mother of young children—that is a huge part of your identity and any attempts to cover that up or overpromise on expectations will leave you running ragged trying to please other people. You will undoubtedly feel like you can never let your guard down."

A job interview is a job interview whether you have children or not. In a single conversation you have to convince someone that your personality, experience, and skills are the best for the job. So do your homework by researching the company and ideally the interviewer. Practice, come in with a copy of your résumé and references, and be ready to sell yourself. Jamie reminds us, "Companies want people who bring energy and edge, and your experiences as a mother can bring a unique perspective to many corporate circles. The corporate world has made great strides in this area over the last ten years and as women start more companies and assume more responsibilities in corporate America, we expect those strides to continue."

the realities of starting your own business

If you are feeling ready to start your own business, then congratulations! As many of you know by now, we love being entrepreneurs and wrote our first book in this series about it, *The Girl's Guide to Starting Your Own Business*. Being an entrepreneur includes everything good and everything bad about business. There are challenges to keep you engaged, conflicts to keep you on your toes, opportunities to keep you passionate, and successes to keep you confident. And while you may find yourself frustrated, anxious, and exhausted, you will never be bored. Ever. The absolute best thing about starting a business? It's all yours. You can create a company and culture that is a true reflection of you. Oh, and you have more control of your income, growth, and future, which is really amazing.

Ask yourself if this is the best time to step out on your own. Follow the steps we outlined in our first book, starting with asking yourself if you have the desire, money, focus, time, and endurance to be an entrepreneur. Not everyone wants to be the one wearing all of the hats and that's fine. Just know that before you quit your job. Check in with your family to see if they're on board with you taking this major step. A new business is a lot like a newborn in that it requires lots of love and attention that may call for sacrifices in other areas of your life. And you don't want to have to make the choice between your two babies. You also want to be clear about what type of business suits your skills, budget, and lifestyle. If you have a one-year-old at home and your spouse is on the road a lot, then opening a retail store that will require your physical presence is a bad idea. If you have preschoolers who need to be picked up at 5 p.m. each night, then you might want to consider a consulting business rather than a restaurant.

Look closely at your personal budget before doing anything. If you have debt as well as a big monthly nut, then think about starting your business on the side for additional income. If you are financially healthy, then figure out how much buffer you have to start your business and get it up and running before taking a salary. And what about that start-up money? Now that you know how much you need to make in the first year, figure out how much your business needs to get off the ground. Make decisions about when to launch and what to launch once you know the financial landscape, because it will impact your next steps. If you have no capital, then what about a consulting or other service-based business that doesn't require huge overhead? If that's the direction you want to go, then do you have the contacts and reputation for that type of business, which is mostly driven by word of mouth? If you are committed to doing a business that requires a significant investment upfront, then how are you at fund-raising? Remember, even if you are asking your best friend for money, she will most likely want and need a business plan to review so that should be what you do before any ask.

As you can see, starting a business is complicated. There are a million questions to ask yourself and professionals, but don't let that stop you from pursuing your dreams. For working moms the question often comes down not to "Can I do this?" but "Can I do this right now?" Just know that it is extremely hard work with a potentially bigger payoff down the road emotionally, professionally, and financially.

a few words from mompreneur Sarah Rubenstein:

Before Sarah Rubenstein went out on her own to found Modern-Tots (www.moderntots.com), she found herself a working mom trying to make her career still work in a working mom–unfriendly corporate environment. We spoke to her about the signs it was time to go and how becoming a mother gave her the confidence to launch her own business.

You are the mother of a six-year-old and the founder of Modern-Tots. How did that business come about?

My decision to start my own company was absolutely influenced by becoming a mother. The unique, modern children's products I was looking for to use in my home with my son just weren't readily available. So I set out to find them and then to create a resource to make them available for other parents.

What about the emotional changes that impacted your decision to become an entrepreneur?

There was something about becoming a mother that made me stronger and braver, and gave me the tenacity to be able to start and run a company of my own.

You were in advertising when you got pregnant. What was it like for you?

While I was pregnant I was not treated any differently than any other staff member. I was expected to travel, stay on my feet for hours, and work until late at night just as I did before. Always an aggressive corporate climber, I was no longer considered to be as capable as my single counterparts once I had my son. People who left before 8 p.m. received dirty looks and comments in the boardroom the next day. It was not permissible to be out of the office due to a sick child.

Did it get worse?

It came to a point where I did not display photographs of my son in my office because it was not only a reminder to me of who I wished I was with, but it was in effect a demotion. This seemed to be true only for the women in the office, because the fathers proudly displayed their family photos around their offices and on their desks.

How have you decided to do things differently now that you run a business?

I'm proud to employ working mothers and strongly believe it is the individual choice to be dedicated to their job and has nothing to do with being a mother or not. The culture here is different from other companies in that we support them as much as we can, including welcoming children into the office.

the word

A JOB-SHARING STORY FROM LINDA CONNOLLY, CO-OWNER OF DAHLIA SITE SELECTION & EVENTS

When we first met Linda she was job sharing a promotions position at a national magazine. She and her job-share partner Mendy Brannon had such a great rapport that they eventually decided to quit the magazine and open a business together.

Why did you decide to look for a job-share position?

My job-share partner and I were both looking for new careers, careers that gave us flexibility in our personal lives. As you get older, your priorities change. It was important for me to be able to spend time with my son and family and have time for myself—that's the reason we decided on a job share. We see a job share as two people working in one position giving more to a company, not less: more experience, more work, and more ideas. And having the free time to pursue other opportunities while we work in a position that we both really liked was an ideal situation.

When does a job share work well for all parties?

The secret to a successful job share is finding the right partner. Mendy and I worked together at two different magazines. We developed camaraderie and a partnership. We worked in two different positions but sought advice and ideas from each other on our projects. We each have different strengths and personalities that we would bring to the job share.

What challenges did you encounter while job sharing?
The most difficult aspect of the job share situation is relaying information. From the beginning, we were very conscious that our coworkers should not have to repeat anything. We had to develop a system that would keep us updated and informed of each other's work. This took extra time and work, and frequently we would speak to each other on our days off, but the luxury of having the flexibility was worth it.

things to know if you decide to opt out

If you have decided that you want to be a stay-at-home mom, we congratulate you for following your heart and making a decision that is right for you. Before closing your office door there are a few things you should prepare yourself for. If you think there is any chance that you will return to the workforce in a year, five years, or ten years, then while you are home protect and nurture your career. If you find after a year that you want to or have to go back to work but haven't picked up a phone to call anyone from your professional life during that time, you're starting from scratch. If you haven't kept on top of changes in your industry or technology, then even if you left as a senior person you're at a disadvantage when going up against other candidates for a job.

Too many of the women we interviewed who had transitioned from home back to work struggled with major confidence issues. Tragically, we were told by women who had given their all to their children and communities that they felt they hadn't done anything worth bringing up in an interview. One woman had raised thousands of dollars for her children's school during her time out of the rat race, but still she told us that she didn't know what to put on her résumé. We recently interviewed someone for a job as our office manager who had taken a year off to deal with her son's medical issues. She spent much of the time focused on her earlier jobs and skimmed over the twelve months that she was organizing doctor appointments, scheduling tutors, researching specialists. It was only when she started talking about those aspects of her year that she began to make sense as a hire for us.

Don't undervalue or undersell what you do as you are raising your children. Being paid is nice, but volunteering can be just as stressful and require you to utilize or hone the skills you had developed while in the workforce. So while you are away, keep track of your accomplishments just as you do now. On a final note, when you are ready to start looking and interviewing, put your activities and contributions into work-speak.

A few ways to nurture your career while you are at home:

- Maintain your network.
- Keep on top of cultural trends that impact your industry.
- Be up on current events.
- Read trade magazines and Web sites.
- If possible, put your skills to work in your community.
- Keep in touch with your mentor.
- Train yourself on new technology.

advice from someone who has been on both sides

Gail Mangurian was a teacher for many years before deciding to become a stay-at-home mom to raise her children. As someone who has worked both inside and outside of the house, she wanted to share this advice with all of us.

These days my twenty-three-year-old daughter is very involved in her marketing career. She is working hard and enjoying her achievements. I am proud of her and what she is doing, and I encourage her to pursue her dreams. My advice to her and all the young women who are entering the workplace or changing career paths would be to . . . follow your heart. Try to get in touch with what your intuition is telling you is right for you. Keep in mind that the heart can lead in different directions for different people. It is my fervent hope that my daughter and other young women will have a legitimate choice between working outside the home and staying at home to raise a family. It seems more difficult than ever to resist the societal pressures placed on women to have full-time careers outside the home. What is politically correct is often not what is right for the individual. How wonderful that there is such a wide spectrum of opportunities for young women nowadays. I hope that they will support each other's differing choices and encourage each other to listen to what the heart is saying.

girl talk

LYNN ABRAMS

Our friend Lynn Abrams is one of the smartest, most ambitious women we know, a go-getter with a top job at a national magazine. When she had her second child we were all prepared for her to happily jump back into the professional pool, but a series of situations made her look at her decisions and choices a little differently.

So you have two children and recently had your third. Around the time your first two were three and one you made a major decision about the structure of your job. Can you tell us about your decision?

When my family and I moved out of New York City to a nearby sub-urb last year, I started commuting to work five days a week, an hour and a half each way. The commute quickly became a grind: I was leaving the house at 8 a.m. and returning at 8 p.m. By the time I got home at night, our full-time nanny had already put the baby down, and my three-year-old was ready for bed. I wasn't seeing my chil-dren, and I was missing out on those (mostly) precious toddler years. To complicate matters, I didn't love the child care my kids were get-ting. I felt that if I was at least working from home, a nanny would be more on her toes, and less likely to, say, plop my kids in front of the TV for hours at a time. I thought the best decision for me would be to work from home full-time. Working from home full-time wasn't something I thought my boss would ever go for. In fact, before I ac-cepted my current position as a magazine editor, I had requested to work from home one day a week, and my boss shot me down. So it's surprising that I eventually got what I wanted—and more.

Were you concerned about how working from home would im-pact the growth of your career?
Yes. In fact, just moving out of the city made me feel like less of a player. Instead of going out for drinks with coworkers or busi-ness associates, I was running for the train. Once I stopped going into the city altogether, it meant giving up a lot of chances to at-tend movie premieres and have spontaneous lunches with high-powered publicists, editors, and writers. I told myself that, for now, my career was just going to move along in a straight line. For the next few years while the kids were young, I would not be making any professional advances. It was definitely a trade-off.

Was it a difficult decision to make?
In the end, no. The commute was exhausting, and I was missing my kids. By working from home, I got to keep my career (more or less) *and* be an at-home mom. It was the perfect place to be at this point in my life.

How did you approach "the ask" with your boss?
After four months of commuting, I set up a meeting with my boss and told her I was quitting. That I needed to be around more to

watch my kids grow up and make sure they were okay. My plan was that I would pursue a career as a full-time freelance editor and work from home. That's when my boss completely shocked me and made me an offer I couldn't refuse. She told me I could keep my job and benefits and work full-time from home. It was like winning the lottery. I wouldn't have to chase down work as a freelancer, and I could be around enough to see my kids.

What compromises did you have to make for this to work?

Even if it was her idea, she put plenty of safeguards into place to make sure the arrangement worked for her. I had to pay out of my own pocket to set up a home office, complete with all the software that would be compatible with my work office. I had to be at my desk and available from nine to six, in case she ever wanted to do an impromptu phone conference. And she had me become a member of a free video conference service, so that when we did have conference calls, she could actually see me at my desk (and, I suspect, make sure I wasn't working in my pajamas). There were times where it felt like Big Brother was watching me, which was disconcerting, to say the least.

How was transitioning to working from home?

It took me a good three months to get used to working from home. It was crucial that I had a separate office, where I could shut the door and not hear the goings-on of the household. (I also put up a baby gate, so the kids couldn't come flying into my office during, say, a phone meeting with my boss.) The challenge was creating an environment in my home where I could focus on my work. Creating the right environment helped me make the mental shift into work mode, even if I wasn't exactly making the physical shift into a corporate office. It was a challenging transition for my kids too. They needed to learn that even though mommy was home, I wasn't available to them (unless, of course, it was an emergency). So just like I did when I would leave for the train, I would tell my kids at 9 a.m., "Mommy is going to work now." And then at noon I'd pop out and have lunch with them. They quickly grasped that mommy had work time, while they had play time with the nanny. But the good news was that at 6:00 p.m., when the work day was over, I had a one-minute commute to the playroom upstairs, and I got to be with my kids.

Do you miss the office environment?

There are times when I go into the city once a week for an important lunch or meeting. That gives me my fix of office gossip and getting dressed up, which I *really* miss. Believe it or not, it's not always fun wearing shorts and T-shirts to work five days a week. Sometimes putting on a suit or Jimmy Choos helps shift you into work mode and gives you a level of confidence that you don't get by wearing slippers. That said, I actually find that I get more work done at home than in an office environment. When a coworker isn't spontaneously dropping by your office for an hour-long gossip session, you actually work.

Is there anything you would have done differently?

Sometimes I wonder if going freelance would have been the best overall solution. Even though this arrangement has allowed me to see my kids a few more hours a day, and to basically know what's going on inside the house with our nanny, etc., I am still beholden to my office between the hours of 9:00 a.m. and 6:00 p.m. It's not like I can take my daughter to a play date and not work for a couple of hours in the afternoon. I have to be available, just like I would be in an office. And that can be extremely stressful. If I were freelance, I could set my own schedule a little bit more and carve out even more time for my children. Sounds ideal, but the money and benefits wouldn't be nearly as steady as they are now.

Do you have any advice for readers thinking about approaching their boss with the request to work from home?

If working from home or part-time is something you really feel strongly about, you ultimately need to be prepared to leave your full-time position if your boss won't allow you to make a shift. But the key is helping your boss understand that a work-from-home situation is achievable (for most jobs, not all, of course). As long as you're willing to come into your office for key meetings, lunches, etc., there's little reason why someone can't make phone calls and do computer work from a satellite location. You just need to be able to lay out your work-from-home plan so your employer understands you can accomplish all the work you do now . . . and maybe more. You can also offer to do it on a trial basis. See if they'll let you work from home for three months before they have to sign up for the idea. If you make a seamless transition to the home office, they'll have little reason not to allow you to make a full-time change. Finding precedence within your company also helps. Do a little research. Who in your corporation is successfully working from home? Give those names to your boss, with their superiors' contact information. Your boss may feel more comfortable giving you the green light if he or she doesn't have to break new ground within the company.

the new you

Now that you have the tools and inspiration to be the best mom *you* can be and now that we have a president and first lady committed to family issues, it's also a good time to consider how you can help other working moms. We have never been so proud and inspired as when we read that Harvard-educated, powerful attorney, and hospital administrator Michelle Obama was taking time out during her husband's historic presidency to be "Mom in Chief." She plans to dedicate their time in office to raising her children and helping working women get the resources they need for their children to thrive. She is choosing to stay home so the rest of us have an opportunity to work. Please don't waste this historic opportunity. If there was ever a time for mothers (working and stay-at-home) to band together, it's now.

our new feminism

In the introduction to her book *Mothers on the Fast Track* (Oxford, 2007), Mary Ann Mason writes: "We know more about why women don't succeed than about how they do." Arlie Hochschild in *The Second Shift* shows that, in spite of women's massive entry into full-time employment, they still bear the burden of family care at home. Ann Crittenden, in *The Wages of Motherhood*, argues that working mothers lose out on economic fronts in large part because our society doesn't value motherhood. And Joan Williams in *Unbending Gender* observes that "the inflexible 'ideal worker' model of the American workplace discriminates against mothers, undermining the purpose of Title VII."

In the face of all of this irrefutable evidence that women have it much harder, what are we supposed to do? Do we just give up? Can any of us afford to opt out? And do we want to? We love working and we shouldn't have to give it up. Men don't. While we've always considered ourselves feminists, our feminism was of the decidedly dormant variety. To be honest, we were more concerned with gay rights than we ever were with women's rights. Unlike our gay friends, we never felt discriminated against *until* we had children.

Becoming working mothers and writing this book has awakened our political fervor. We work because it's our right to work and be mothers. After you have children, it becomes all too obvious that women are pressured to make sacrifices and choices—and judged by society for them—that men don't. And the more we think about it, the more stridently feminist we become.

In her revolutionary one-hundred-page book, *Get to Work: A Manifesto for Women of the World* (Viking, 2006), philosopher, feminist, and retired professor Linda Hirshman calls all women into the workplace—because that's where the power is. She offers a "Strategic Plan to Get to Work" that's a bit extreme but gets us thinking. Here it is:

- Don't study art. Use your education to prepare for a lifetime of work.
- Never quit a job until you have another one. Take work seriously.
- Never know when you're out of milk. Bargain relentlessly for a just household.
- Consider a reproductive strike.
- Get the government you deserve. Stop electing governments that punish women's work.

We're all in, except for the reproductive strike. If women don't stand up and ask for a fair deal on the home front, they will never get one. Until men are forced to make the same choices and sacrifices we do, things will never change. AUTHOR'S NOTE: We promise that we won't return to the soapbox until our next book.

the word

CATHERINE WOLFRAM AND THE OPT-OUT OPTION

Catherine Wolfram is an associate professor of economics at the University of California, Berkeley, Haas School of Business. She earned her Ph.D. in economics from M.I.T. and did her undergraduate work at Harvard. As a tenured professor in a highly competitive university, she is on the "fast track," as defined by her colleague and author Mary Ann Mason in her book *Mothers on the Fast Track* (Oxford, 2007). Like many fast-track women, she is married to a Ph.D. whom she met in graduate school. She is also the mother of two children. Like top corporate jobs, coveted tenured positions at universities are mainly populated by men. Academia is not widely considered a family-friendly environment, although you can create a flexible schedule. A colleague of Catherine's is fond of saying, "Academia gives you the flexibility to work whichever sixteen hours of the day you'd like."

To understand Catherine's story, we need to take a moment to explain tenure. Achieving tenure is the Holy Grail in academia because it guarantees a scholar the right to research and publish any interest, whether or not it conflicts with the university's policies. Without tenure, academics would focus on keeping their jobs, not discovery. Achieving tenure is a rigorous and political process. You are literally on the clock. A tenure-track professor has six years to gain a national reputation with publication while teaching classes and winning research grants to fund studies.

Once again, studies (including one authored by Mason) have shown that it's much more difficult for women to achieve tenure than men. Unfortunately, the biological and tenure clocks are ticking on the same schedule. The average professor achieves tenure at forty. On average, you have as many as six years to earn it. The more prestigious the university, the more competitive the tenure process is, and it usually requires the entire six years to complete. You don't have to be a math whiz like Catherine to figure this one out. If you finish your Ph.D. in your early thirties, the six years you are working toward tenure are the six years you've got left to create a family.

As a matter of fact, the percentage of tenured women professors is so disturbingly low versus the Ph.D.s awarded to women that, in 2005, nine top universities, including Berkeley, adopted policies to make tenure more family friendly, including offering extensions of the tenure clock in the event of childbirth or adoption, and generous leave or relief from teaching.

When Catherine got pregnant in her sixth year, she opted to stop her tenure clock during her maternity leave even though she had finished most of the required work. While she was out, she received a tenure offer from another university. As Berkeley was her first choice, she gave them an opportunity to make her a counteroffer. However, technically she wasn't qualified to sit for the tenure at Berkeley because she had chosen to delay the clock for her maternity leave. She wasn't asking for special allowances, she was just asking to be evaluated on her regular schedule. The university refused. With the full support of the business school, she spent two months fighting the system and was eventually awarded her tenure.

Remember, the great thing about tenure is that you can study anything that interests you. Normally Catherine's research focuses on energy markets. One day while flipping through her Harvard alumni newsletter, she noticed a high number of women graduates who had opted out of the labor force to raise children. So she decided to study the issue. Now as important as her energy studies are, the general public had taken little interest when they were published; not so with the publication of "Opt-Out Patterns Across Careers: Labor Force Participation Among Highly Educated Mothers," co-authored with Jane Leber Herr.

Catherine and Jane followed the career paths of nearly one thousand women who graduated from Harvard between 1988 and 1991, using a rich set of biographical data culled from tenth- and fifteenth-anniversary reunion surveys. Their work showed that by the time the graduates are fifteen years out of college, 28 percent of the Harvard women who went on to get their M.B.A.s were stay-at-home moms, compared to only 6 percent of women who got medical degrees. The study also looked at the career paths of Harvard women who became lawyers and found 21 percent chose to stay home with their children.

The reasons why more M.B.A.s opt out may speak to the differences in the family-friendliness of the fields. Catherine and Jane's statistics show these women have the financial ability to opt out, but also they are in careers with very little flexibility in a culture that is still male dominated and would never be confused with being family friendly. For these women to spend any time with their families, opting out may seem like the only choice. Doctors, on the other hand, are doing "good" work and can eventually set a more flexible schedule and the lawyers often have too much loan debt to have a choice at all.

So the rich and successful choose to stay home to raise their children? Big deal. They can afford it. Harvard women tend to marry highly educated and well-paid men, giving these women the *option* of staying home, which many women in the population don't have. Also, many Harvard women have accrued their own wealth (through family or prior earnings), again offering them the *option* to opt out when other women wouldn't.

Why should the rest of us care? We can't afford to leave our jobs (and we really don't want to anyway). We must care because these fast-track women are exactly the ones we need to keep in the labor pool. They are the ones most likely to rise to a level in business where they can make decisions that help other working women and make the necessary changes that include paid maternity leave, flexible schedules, and affordable health care.

One final disturbing thought from the press release about Catherine and Jane's study: "Another consideration is that many of these women are married to men who are just as ambitious as they are," said Joan Williams, director of the Center for WorkLife Law at the University of California and an expert on work and family life issues.

Williams said she believes that what has been termed the "opt-out revolution," the notion that working women choose parenting over building their careers, is more complicated than meets the eye. Men who are in the upper ranks of their profession with stay-at-home wives earn 30 percent more than men who are married to women who work, she said. Those men who want to reach the highest rungs of their career and earn the most money often need a stay-at-home wife to take care of all other aspects of their life, including raising a family, Williams said. "And since many women in business school marry those men, they end up being stay-at-home wives, regardless of their own vision of what they wanted from their careers."

WHO'S GETTING IT RIGHT

It's not all bad news. Many companies have realized that making the workplace more supportive for working women is not just the right thing to do, but good business. As we mentioned in Chapter One, *Working Mother* magazine (www.workingmother.com) features the one hundred best companies for working mothers each year. The criteria for making their best list are stringent and include offering a range of benefits that help working mothers; among them are flextime, financial planning, telecommuting, job sharing, domestic partner benefits, prenatal programs, and paid adoption leave. If you are on the job search, we encourage you to go to the *Working Mother* site to read more about these companies. If you are a manager or small business owner, we encourage you to consider adopting a few of the benefits that are so important to working mothers.

The 2007 Working Mothers Top Ten Best Companies:
1. Baptist Health South Florida
2. Booz Allen Hamilton
3. Ernst & Young
4. General Mills
5. IBM
6. KPMG
7. The McGraw-Hill Companies
8. PricewaterhouseCoopers
9. UBS
10. Wachovia

the word

Kingsley Shannon is a senior manager of brand services for Calphalon and lives in Atlanta with her husband and two children, one and five years old. Her five-year-old son was born while she was a brand manager at Maytag in Iowa. Kingsley had an excellent employment record at Maytag. She had developed a reputation as a conscientious employee and strong leader. Her managers and team liked and respected her.

Prior to getting pregnant, Kingsley had watched how a number of other women handled their pregnancies and maternity leave. She had a good pregnancy but suffered from high blood pressure, which required her to go to a number of extra doctor's appointments. Her managers subscribed to a philosophy that she employs today: "We're all responsible adults. If you have a doctor's appointment, go and take care of it. We're not watching your hours. Getting the work done is what matters." It wasn't a corporate policy but rather an unwritten agreement between manager and staff member.

Kingsley loved her job, but as with most American families, she needed it to help support her family. So for her, the question of work–life balance came up the second she found out she was pregnant. As with everything else she had done before professionally, she decided to make a plan and stick to it.

It began with preparing for her maternity leave. As the team leader, she found it relatively easy to set the strategy in advance and created a detailed project list that outlined where and how everything was running. She set it up so that from an executional standpoint it could run without her. She had a strong number two and a great outside agency partner who she empowered to make decisions in her absence. She cleared the budgets with her senior management, downloaded a complete project status, and made it clear that she would not be checking in during her maternity leave.

She planned to be out for twelve weeks. Maytag paid in full for eight because she had a cesarean, and she used vacation for two weeks and took two weeks unpaid leave. Kingsley went back to work but missed her son more than even she anticipated. Her son was in in-home day care from 7:30 in the morning until 5:30 in the evening. And she missed him and started looking for ways to maximize her time with him. She either worked through lunch or went to visit him, and except in the extreme case, walked out the door at 5:00 p.m. She was still unsatisfied. She wanted more time.

Maytag had no corporate policy for flex-hours, although over the years she had heard whispers that it was happening. When Jack was nine months old, she asked her manager for permission to work four ten-hour days and take Fridays off. Her commitment to them (and what ultimately got it approved) was that if there was ever a time that they felt she was out of the office too much, then she would come back. It wasn't a program that went through human resources; it was a privilege that she was granted from management because of her strong track record and their desire to keep her as an employee.

It went very well. She worked four ten-hour days for a little more than two years when she was promoted to a different division. The new manager was willing to give it a trial (even though, as she puts it, "he wasn't normally an active work–life balance guy") and then evaluate. She made the same commitment: If there was ever a time that they felt her missing, then she would come back. She never had to go back.

As a manager, she was able to set up the workflow so that her team was working on things that didn't require her input on Fridays. She scheduled all of her meetings between Monday and Thursday. She checked in from home during nap time on Fridays.

She had been at Maytag for eight years and earned their trust. They knew she was an asset and a responsible employee. In her first year with Jack, she learned what her work-balance threshold was and set her boundaries accordingly. And she stuck to them with no guilt. Kingsley noted, "Many women I talk to feel like they can't say no, and are always feeling guilty. I don't."

Now Kingsley is at Calphalon, back to working five days a week, albeit on flex hours. It's not her ideal, but she gets in at 7 a.m. and tries to leave at 4 p.m. to beat the traffic. She's still firm in her boundaries and travels or stays late only when she absolutely must. She'd still love to be home with her kids, but she also loves her job and the new challenges and opportunities it has presented her. And she feels proud that she can support her family.

In the beginning, everyone was skeptical, but by the end they all had the same question, "How did you do it?"

Kingsley shares some tips for how to do it:

- Create a work-balance ideal and work toward it. Be very clear about what your desires are. Set boundaries and do not apologize. And don't feel guilty. You need to take your daughter to the doctor, and you need to get work done. They shouldn't be mutually exclusive. In most cases, over-delivering on the work front awards you more freedom. And experience breeds success. If you're able to run out for a couple of errands and still get all of your work done, your manager knows it and you both gain confidence and build trust from that interaction. But if the work suffers, then it's a completely different story. You win a work-life balance only if you give enough on the work front.
- Both your employer *and* your family need to feel like you are trying to balance. You have to be reasonable with your employer. Don't expect them to bend over backward to accommodate your personal life. Pick and choose your spots. Make a decision and don't ask for everything.
- Assess your priorities and figure out what you want to spend your money on. I decided when I had Jack to hire a cleaning lady once a week, and it was the best money I ever spent. For me it was more important to get home and have quality time with my kids than to have a night out with another couple. We are willing to pay for convenience so I can have more time with our kids.
- Don't be available to your employer 24/7. BlackBerry is great for me. I leave at 4:00 p.m. and check e-mail up till

close of business and tie up any loose ends. After business hours and on weekends, I *choose* if I want to look at it and catch up before getting into the office. (Sometimes I make the mental decision that it is family time and I am not looking at it until after the kids are in bed or Saturday afternoon.) I typically make it a practice not to respond after business hours unless it is an absolute emergency. If I do respond it is because I know I am going to have a busy day and won't have time in the morning *or* because I am managing my workload on my time outside of the hours I am in the office. People know I do not conduct business on Saturday because I have set the expectation of not responding to their weekend queries. I read a lot that comes through but wait until I am at work during business hours to respond.

role, not runway, models

Every day we read about the celebrity supermoms featured in those trashy (but delicious) magazines. And you know what we see? Beautiful and accomplished women, back to their pre-baby—oh heck, pre-puberty weight—three weeks after giving birth. We see them storming through airport security, with guards and nannies in tow. We see $100,000 baby-room renovations, and cashmere-themed baby showers hosted by the Jennifer Garners of the world. Sure, it's fun to take a sneak peek inside an assistant-supported world, but that isn't our life. And it isn't the life of most everyone we know. Working mom Arianne Weeks agrees: "I do feel the media creates unrealistic role models—celebrities and otherwise. But that goes along with a perfectionist attitude that is rampant in our culture. So many of us experience a constant feeling that there is a right and wrong way to be doing everything and motherhood is a part of that."

The realistic role models for working moms might be sitting in the conference room during your weekly meeting. Their lives may not be as glamorous, and they may still be carrying a few baby pounds and have decided to live with their wrinkles instead of Botoxing them away, but anyone managing to be a great mother while taking care of herself and her career is now your role model. Believe us, these women have invaluable systems for running their lives learned through trial and error and real-life experience. Rather than look to the "Just Like Us!" pages, ask the real women around you how they get their kids off to school in the morning.

The American Academy of Pediatrics states on its Web site: "A mother who successfully manages both an outside job and parenthood provides a role model for her child. In most families with working mothers, each person plays a more active role in the household. The children tend to look after one another and help in other ways. The father is more likely to help with household chores and child rearing as well as breadwinning. These positive outcomes are most likely when the working mother feels valued and supported by family, friends, and coworkers."

You may not like it, or have ever planned for it, but as a working mother you are a role model not just for your children but for other women in your organization. How you manage your work and family will be carefully watched by the women coming up the ladder behind you. When surveyed, the number one question young career women ask is, "When is the best time to have a baby?" Of course we know now the answer is there is never a good time to have a baby. You just figure it out as you go along—hopefully with the help of this book.

As a working mother role model we encourage you to be honest about the challenges that you face. If asked, be honest with women about the challenges of working motherhood. Help them navigate their pregnancy and maternity leaves professionally and proactively. Welcome them back and be supportive when they have a hard time—because you know they will have a hard time.

Also, you can work within your organization to change policies that negatively affect working women. If they don't offer flextime as a corporate policy, then do it within your own department and share the successful results with management.

get active and political

If the election of 2008 proved anything, it's that change is possible if we become part of the democratic process. Big business will not change until the government requires it to, so we have to actively lobby government to support issues that affect working mothers and their families. Write your congressman to support the family leave bills that are stuck in committee. Work with your human resources department to make changes in policy. As the country's upcoming leaders, you have a responsibility to speak up and try to effect change. Go online and research the working mother advocacy organizations (there are lots of them now) and volunteer. You can make a difference if you want to. Betty's story certainly shows that.

girl talk

THE MORE THINGS CHANGE . . .

Betty Holcomb was a thirty-five-year-old successful freelance writer when she became pregnant with her first child in 1984. As she expected, becoming a mother was the life-changing event that everybody warned her it would be. What she didn't expect was that her professional life was going to change dramatically too.

In theory, she had a great setup. As a freelance writer, she could maintain a flexible schedule. She would still need child care (her salary was a necessity to her family, and as a freelancer, if you don't work, you don't get paid) and she set about to find some.

It's important to set the stage for working mothers in the eighties. It may be clichéd now, but in 1984 the image of the woman wearing the power suit holding a briefcase in one hand and the baby in the other was the reality. In 1984, pregnancy discrimination was all too real. Most employers expected women to stay home after they gave birth and so summarily firing them when they announced their pregnancies was not uncommon. Remember, the Pregnancy Discrimination Act was not passed until 1986!

Working motherhood was becoming a national issue in the eighties, and not only had Betty just joined the ranks of working moms, she was being assigned high-profile magazine pieces about the subject, including a cover story for *New York* magazine. Huge debates about national funding for child care began, and there was a lot of romance about how women entering the workplace could balance work and family and actually have it all. (Sound familiar?)

Like other women who began working in the wake of the women's movement of the seventies, Betty believed the hype. She thought women could have it all without sacrificing their careers. She believed that her husband would contribute 50 percent to the parenting and domestic issues. She believed that safe, affordable child care would be easy to find, and the workplace would welcome women back after maternity leave, so she could continue the career in which she had already invested fifteen years.

So it was nothing short of stunning to her, when on assignment for *Savvy* magazine about women returning from maternity leave, she began calling women in management at major corporations and heard them sobbing to her about their experiences. She was the first person with whom many of these women had shared their stories, and their stories were all the same. They felt isolated and pushed aside at work. They were forced to pretend their children didn't exist, fearing plum assignments would be taken away and they would be passed over for promotion. They were marginalized in the workplace and, worse, they felt like they were bad mothers because they chose to return to working and allowed others to care for their children.

That story led to writing regularly for *Working Mother* (a revolutionary publication at the time), and when someone went on maternity leave she took a staff position. *Working Mother* became the right place at the right time to partner with advocacy groups around the issues of women in the workplace. She spent her days researching the companies that were truly "family friendly" and working on the first ever *Working Mother* "100 Best" list.

The combination of being a working mother and her work on the subject turned Betty into a born-again feminist. She enrolled in a graduate program in women's history at Sarah Lawrence College and began writing newsletters for various child advocacy organizations.

Betty has since written two books, *Not Guilty! The Good News for Working Mothers* (Simon & Schuster, 1998) and *The Best Friend's Guide to Maternity Leave* (Perseus, 2001), for which we owe her a debt of gratitude, as we've referred to them both liberally in this book. She's currently the policy director for Child Care, Inc. (CCI), a nonprofit organization that works to expand and improve early care and education across New York State.

Betty's experience, as well as the experience of the hundreds of women she's interviewed, sounds frighteningly familiar. We spoke to her about what has changed in the last twenty years and what we can all do to make the workplace a friendlier place for working women and families.

Your experience in 1984 sounds way too much like our experience in 2008. What has really changed?

It would be really silly to say nothing has changed. I think most Americans today would never say, unequivocally, women shouldn't work. Up until 1986, it was just expected that women would quit their jobs when they got pregnant—no matter if they needed the money. The biggest difference now, though, is that laws protect women from discrimination. You can't understate how important the sexual and pregnancy discrimination laws and the Family Medical Leave Act are for women. You can just point to the issues in the presidential election in 2008. Women and family issues are significant parts of the platforms of both parties.

Also, the quality of and attitude toward early education have completely changed since I had Rachel. The federal child care block grant passed in 1990 supports early education in every state. Study after study has proven that children benefit from early education, so day care centers are no longer stigmatized. When I told people that I had Rachel in an amazing and supportive day care center, I was treated like I was committing child abuse. Now more than 75 percent of preschool-age children are in some form of early development program.

Has anything gotten worse?
I wrote an article in 2000 in *Ms.* magazine called "Friendly for Whose Family," which looked at the distribution for family-friendly benefits and found that the people who need them the least, management, generally are the ones who receive the lion's share of the benefits. If anything, that divide has gotten worse. I have done some research for an update to the story, and it looks like we're going to have to accomplish parity through public policy because employers are more stubborn now that there is a labor surplus.

In times of labor shortages—or in times of labor shortages in emerging industries (high-tech, communications, pharmaceuticals)—companies are actively engaged in trying to recruit and retain workers and therefore very bullish on work-family balance issues. In times of labor surplus, simply put, not so much. When there's no motivation, it's easier to slide back into old grooves and habits, which are employment practices and attitudes that are fundamentally biased toward active parenting.

And, if you look at the statistics, men's engagement in child care and housework has changed the least. Domestic issues are still largely a women's problem.

What can we do to make a change?
For the first time in the major political arena, presidential candidates are talking about early childhood education, and not as an after-thought. It's high up there in the conversation.

Local communities have made huge headway in funding for the early ages and there's a move to expand publicly funded education to include preschool, defined at ages three and four. As a parent you can get involved with your local child care centers and partner with them. You can also vote for national and local representatives who prioritize family issues.

And you can continue to help change the attitudes toward working women. When I had Rachel, everything about my life was determined by the fact that I was a mother. Why are we still making mothers feel guilty about choosing work *and* family?

If there was a romance when I was young, it was about women going into the workplace. The new romance is around women going home and being perfect mothers and homemakers. There is not much at all in the data to indicate that it is actually happening, but it's being romanticized. If anything, once you have children, you feel more need for the additional income and that's where American women are really challenged.

Discrimination is harder for younger women to see. The fact that a woman could be fired for becoming pregnant is an outrage now. But discrimination now is not as black and white. Are you being discriminated against because you are no longer in the running for the big job after becoming a mother?

a final note

The amazing thing about becoming a mother is you just don't know how it is going to affect you. We had a similar experience writing this book. We thought we had all of the answers—we were very, very in touch with both our frustrations and our failures, and thought we had created systems to work smarter. We also demanded support on the home front.

But the more interviews we did and the more studies we read, the more we realized that we're still very much a work in progress, too. The women's stories that we share in this book all taught us important lessons about time management and the importance of planning ahead, but what really struck us was that the women who were really flourishing in both roles had two things in common: (1) they settled for good enough and (2) they had a supportive partner *or* hired a supportive infrastructure to share the load. Good partners or nannies seem to be the key to success, because they mitigate the mother guilt. Penelope Trunk said it best: "women can't be good at their jobs if they don't trust that their children are being cared for properly." And that's the secret.

If you can go to work trusting (and that is a loaded word on purpose) that your children are safe and loved, then you miss only a couple of beats at work when you return from maternity leave. If you have ongoing stresses and pressures about the kids' well-being, then it's really hard to do a good job.

And after hearing more times than we can count during the writing of this book statements like "I'm trying to juggle my work and family" and "I'm looking to achieve a work/life balance," we're going to go out on a limb and recommend you give up on both of those goals. Right now.

You're not a circus performer. The art of juggling takes years to perfect and, frankly, you don't have the time. Look at it another way: Even the most accomplished jugglers drop the ball sometimes. Do you really want to choose what hits the ground—your career or your family? You don't control enough factors in your work or your family life to keep the balance. One sick kid and there it goes. We're visual thinkers. We don't like to think about our balls hitting the ground or our butts slamming down when the seesaw goes out of balance.

So instead of juggling, try aiming for harmony instead. The goal is to get all parts of your life into agreement, and that requires communication and negotiation at home and at work. And remember, your life isn't written in stone. The most professionally identified woman we know has decided to become a stay-at-home mom, while another who swore to us she would *never* put her child in day care decided to do just that three weeks into her maternity leave. If you find yourself going back to work and loving it, you may still desire to change your schedule, gravitate toward different projects, or make a career change.

So the lesson is keep an open mind, and start training yourself to cut down and cut back—you can't do it all. We know, easier said than done, but start taking steps. Choose one hour of your day and focus on one thing only. If you choose work, pick a task and immerse yourself in it completely. Don't check e-mail. Don't answer the phone. Don't chat with someone. Just complete the task with full focus. We guarantee you will be amazed by two things: (1) the speed with which the task gets completed and (2) how happy you are with the final product. Little by little, start applying it to all aspects of your life. But start slowly. It's very difficult to make a paradigm shift all at once. Your goal is to stop juggling everything by the end of three months.

Motherhood is one of the most profound experiences you can have and it will change you in infinite ways. As with any major life upheaval, it will inspire you to take stock of what you want and what you value. Take the opportunity to evaluate your goals and priorities. Get to know yourself and the job you're in a little better. Are you comfortable blurring the lines between work and home or do you need to establish stricter boundaries? How important is your job? What do you want out of your professional life now? Do you want to pull back from your career or put in more energy?

As you are getting used to working while parenting, you want to keep open all options available to you. You also want to maintain a solid relationship and great reputation so you can negotiate from a position of strength should you decide to make a professional change.

Ultimately, we hope this book gave you the tools and inspiration you need to be the most capable, confident, and fulfilled working mother you can be.

Good luck. We're rooting for you.

resources

RESEARCH

- *Not Guilty!: The Good News for Working Mothers* by Betty Holcomb
- *The Best Friend's Guide to Maternity Leave* by Betty Holcomb
- *Down Came the Rain: My Journey Through Post-Partum Depression* by Brooke Shields
- The U.S. Equal Employment Opportunity Commission, the government agency in charge of administering and enforcing the Pregnancy Discrimination Act: http://www.eeoc.gov/facts/fs-preg.html
- Americans with Disabilities Act: http://www.ada.gov/
- U.S. Department of Labor/Family Medical Leave Act: http://www.dol.gov/esa/whd/fmla/
- www.babycenter.com
- www.wikipedia.com
- *Working Mother:* www.workingmother.com
- MomsRising: www.momsrising.org

- Center for Work and the Family: www.centerforworkand family.com
- Kaiser Family Foundation: www.kff.org
- Sloan Work and Family Research Network: http://wfnetwork.bc.edu/
- U.S. Office of Personnel Management: www.opm.gov
- Council on Accreditation: www.coa.org
- Child Care Inc.: www.childcareinc.org
- www.kidshealth.org
- National Association for the Education of Young Children: www.naeyc.org

CAREER ADVICE

- *A Manager's Guide to Hiring the Best Person for Every Job* by DeAnne Rosenberg
- *The Girl's Guide to Starting Your Own Business* by Caitlin Friedman and Kimberly Yorio
- *The Girl's Guide to Being a Boss Without Being a Bitch* by Caitlin Friedman and Kimberly Yorio
- *The Girl's Guide to Kicking Your Career into Gear* by Caitlin Friedman and Kimberly Yorio
- www.monster.com
- www.ycmedia.com
- www.girlsguidetobusiness.com
- www.flexibleexecutives.com

FINANCIAL ADVICE

- *My Money Matters Kit* by Galia Gichon
- www.downtoearthfinance.com
- www.kiplinger.com
- www.money.com
- www.geezo.com

- www.wesabe.com
- www.mint.com

SUPPORT/SOCIAL NETWORKING

- www.workitmom.com
- www.momlogic.com
- www.workingmomsagainstguilt.com
- www.workingmomsblog.com
- www.divinecaroline.com

PRODUCTS

- Modern Tots: www.moderntots.com
- Ingrid and Isabel: www.ingridandisabel.com
- www.babystyle.com